W9-CEJ-252

The Firm
the Market
and the Law

The Firm
the Market
and the Law

R. H. Coase

The University of Chicago Press
Chicago and London

The University of Chicago Press, Chicago 60637
The University of Chicago Press, Ltd., London
© 1988 by The University of Chicago
All rights reserved. Published 1988
Paperback edition 1990
Printed in the United States of America

04 03 02 01 00 99 98 97 96 95   6 7 8 9 10

Library of Congress Cataloging-in-Publication Data

Coase, R. H. (Ronald Harry)
    The firm, the market, and the law/R. H. Coase.
    Includes index.
    ISBN 0-226-11101-6 (paper)
    1. Industrial organization (Economic theory)   2. Externalities
(Economics)   3. Capitalism.   I. Title.
HD2326.C6   1988
338.5'142—dc19   87-24193

♾ The paper used in this publication meets the minimum
requirements of the American National Standard for Information
Sciences—Permanence of Paper for Printed Library Materials,
ANSI Z39.48-1984.

Contents

Preface
vii

ONE
The Firm, the Market, and the Law
1

TWO
The Nature of the Firm
33

THREE
Industrial Organization: A Proposal for Research
57

FOUR
The Marginal Cost Controversy
75

FIVE
The Problem of Social Cost
95

SIX
Notes on the Problem of Social Cost
157

SEVEN
The Lighthouse in Economics
187

Index
215

Preface

The purpose of this book is to persuade my fellow economists to change the way they analyze a number of important questions in micro-economics. Most of the book consists of reprints of previously published articles, but I have attempted in an introductory essay and in a paper entitled "Notes on the Problem of Social Cost" to make clearer the character of the argument in these articles and to respond to some of the main criticisms which have been made of them.

No changes have been made in the articles reprinted except to correct misprints and to remove some eccentricities in my spelling and grammar.

I have to thank Gary Becker, Gerhard Casper, Aaron Director, and George Stigler, all of whom read my introductory essay and "Notes on the Problem of Social Cost" and made suggestions which have resulted in many improvements, although not as many as they would have wished.

ONE

The Firm, the Market, and the Law

I. The Aim of the Book

The core of this book consists of three papers, "The Nature of the Firm" (1937), "The Marginal Cost Controversy" (1946), and "The Problem of Social Cost" (1960). Other papers which extend, illustrate, or explain the arguments in these three papers are also included. As will become apparent, these essays all embody essentially the same point of view.

My point of view has not in general commanded assent, nor has my argument, for the most part, been understood. No doubt inadequacies in my exposition have been partly responsible for this and I am hopeful that this introductory essay, which deals with some of the main points raised by commentators and restates my argument, will help to make my position more understandable. But I do not believe that a failure of exposition is the main reason why economists have found my argument so difficult to assimilate. As the argument in these papers is, I believe, simple, so simple indeed as almost to make their propositions fall into the category of truths which can be deemed self-evident, their rejection or apparent incomprehensibility would seem to imply that most economists have a different way of looking at economic problems and do not share my conception of the nature of our subject. This I believe to be true.

At the present time the dominant view of the nature of economics is that expressed in Robbins' definition: "Economics is the science which studies human behaviour as a relationship between ends and scarce means which have alternative

1

uses."[1] This makes economics the science of human choice. In practice, most economists, including Robbins, restrict their work to a much narrower set of choices than this definition would suggest. Recently, however, Becker has argued that Robbins' way of looking at economics need not be so constrained and that the economic approach, as he terms it, can and should be applied more generally throughout the social sciences. That the economic approach can be applied successfully in the other social sciences is demonstrated by Becker's own work.[2] Its very success, however, poses the question, Why have the economists' tools of trade proved to be so versatile?

My particular interest has been in that part of economic theory which deals with firms, industries, and markets, which used to be called Value and Distribution and is now usually termed price theory or micro-economics. It is an intricate structure of high intellectual quality and has produced valuable insights. Economists study how the choice of consumers, in deciding which goods and services to purchase, is determined by their incomes and the prices at which goods and services can be bought. They also study how producers decide what factors of production to use and what products and services to make and sell and in what quantities, given the prices of the factors, the demand for the final product, and the relation between output and the amounts of factors employed. The analysis is held together by the assumption that consumers maximize utility (a nonexistent entity which plays a part similar, I suspect, to that of ether in the old physics) and by the assumption that producers have as their aim to maximize profit or net income (for which there is a good deal more evidence). The decisions of consumers and producers are brought into harmony by the theory of exchange.

The elaboration of the analysis should not hide from us its essential character: it is an analysis of choice. It is this which gives the theory its versatility. Becker points out that "what

1. Lionel Robbins, *An Essay on the Nature and Significance of Economic Science*, 2nd ed. (London: Macmillan & Co., 1935), 16.

2. See the various studies in Gary S. Becker, *The Economic Approach to Human Behavior* (Chicago: University of Chicago Press, 1976).

most distinguishes economics as a discipline from other disciplines in the social sciences is not its subject matter but its approach."[3] If the theories which have been developed in economics (or at any rate in micro-economics) constitute for the most part a way of analyzing the determinants of choice (and I think this is true), it is easy to see that they should be applicable to other human choices such as those that are made in law or politics. In this sense economists have no subject matter. What has been developed is an approach divorced (or which can be divorced) from subject matter. Indeed, since man is not the only animal that chooses, it is to be expected that the same approach can be applied to the rat, cat, and octopus, all of whom are no doubt engaged in maximizing their utilities in much the same way as does man. It is therefore no accident that price theory has been shown to be applicable to animal behaviour.[4]

This preoccupation of economists with the logic of choice, while it may ultimately rejuvenate the study of law, political science, and sociology, has nonetheless had, in my view, serious adverse effects on economics itself. One result of this divorce of the theory from its subject matter has been that the entities whose decisions economists are engaged in analyzing have not been made the subject of study and in consequence lack any substance. The consumer is not a human being but a consistent set of preferences. The firm to an economist, as Slater has said, "is effectively defined as a cost curve and a demand curve, and the theory is simply the logic of optimal pricing and input combination."[5] Exchange takes place without any specification of its institutional setting. We have consumers without humanity, firms without organization, and even exchange without markets.

The rational utility maximizer of economic theory bears no resemblance to the man on the Clapham bus or, indeed, to

3. Ibid., 5.
4. See, for example, John H. Kagel, Raymond C. Battalio, Howard Rachlin, and Leonard Green, "Demand Curves for Animal Consumers," *Quarterly Journal of Economics* 96, no. 1 (February 1981): 1–14.
5. Martin Slater, Foreword to Edith T. Penrose, *The Theory of the Growth of the Firm*, 2nd ed. (White Plains, N.Y.: M. E. Sharpe, 1980), ix.

any man (or woman) on any bus. There is no reason to suppose that most human beings are engaged in maximizing anything unless it be unhappiness, and even this with incomplete success. Knight has expressed the thought very well: ". . . [the] argument of economists . . . that men work and think to get themselves out of trouble is at least half an inversion of the facts. The things we work for are 'annoyers' as often as 'satisfiers,' we spend as much ingenuity in getting into trouble as in getting out, and in any case enough to keep in effectively. . . . A man who has nothing to worry about immediately busies himself in creating something, gets into some absorbing game, falls in love, prepares to conquer some enemy, or hunt lions or the North Pole or what not."[6]

I believe that human preferences came to be what they are in those millions of years in which our ancestors (whether or not they can be classified as human) lived in hunting bands and were those preferences which, in such conditions, were conducive to survival. It may be, therefore, that ultimately the work of sociobiologists (and their critics) will enable us to construct a picture of human nature in such detail that we can derive the set of preferences with which economists start. And if this result is achieved, it will enable us to refine our analysis of consumer demand and of other kinds of behaviour in the economic sphere. In the meantime, however, whatever makes men choose as they do, we must be content with the knowledge that for groups of human beings, in almost all circumstances, a higher (relative) price for anything will lead to a reduction in the amount demanded. This does not only refer to a money price but to price in its widest sense. Whether men are rational or not in deciding to walk across a dangerous thoroughfare to reach a certain restaurant, we can be sure that fewer will do so the more dangerous it becomes. And we need not doubt that the availability of a less dangerous alternative, say, a pedestrian bridge, will normally reduce the number of those crossing the thoroughfare, nor that, as what is gained by crossing becomes more attractive, the number of people crossing

6. Frank H. Knight, *The Ethics of Competition*, 2nd ed. (New York: Harper & Bros., 1936), 32.

will increase. The generalization of such knowledge constitutes price theory. It does not seem to me to require us to assume that men are rational utility maximizers. On the other hand, it does not tell us why people choose as they do. Why a man will take a risk of being killed in order to obtain a sandwich is hidden from us even though we know that, if the risk is increased sufficiently, he will forego seeking that pleasure.

None of the essays in this book deals with the character of human preferences, nor, as I have said, do I believe that economists will be able to make much headway until a great deal more work has been done by sociobiologists and other noneconomists. But the acceptance by economists of a view of human nature so lacking in content is of a piece with their treatment of institutions which are central to their work. These institutions are the firm and the market which together make up the institutional structure of the economic system. In mainstream economic theory, the firm and the market are, for the most part, assumed to exist and are not themselves the subject of investigation. One result has been that the crucial role of the law in determining the activities carried out by the firm and in the market has been largely ignored. What differentiates the essays in this book is not that they reject existing economic theory, which, as I have said, embodies the logic of choice and is of wide applicability, but that they employ this economic theory to examine the role which the firm, the market, and the law play in the working of the economic system.

II. The Firm

The firm in modern economic theory is an organization which transforms inputs into outputs. Why firms exist, what determines the number of firms, what determines what firms do (the inputs a firm buys and the output it sells) are not questions of interest to most economists. The firm in economic theory, as Hahn said recently, is a "shadowy figure."[7] This lack of interest

7. Frank Hahn, "General Equilibrium Theory," in *The Crisis in Economic Theory*, ed. Daniel Bell and Irving Kristol (New York: Basic Books, 1981), 131.

is quite extraordinary, given that most people in the United States, the United Kingdom, and other western countries are employed by firms, that most production takes place within firms, and that the efficiency of the whole economic system depends to a very considerable extent on what happens within these economic molecules. It was the purpose of my article on "The Nature of the Firm" to provide a rationale for the firm and to indicate what determines the range of activities it undertakes. Although the article has been much cited, it is obvious from such remarks as those of Hahn that the ideas in this article (published about fifty years ago) have not become part and parcel of the equipment of an economist. And it is easy to see why. In order to explain why firms exist and what activities they undertake, I found it necessary to introduce a concept which I termed in that article "the cost of using the price mechanism," "the cost of carrying out a transaction by means of an exchange on the open market," or simply "marketing costs." To express the same idea in my article on "The Problem of Social Cost," I used the phrase "the costs of market transactions." These have come to be known in the economic literature as "transaction costs." I have described what I had in mind in the following terms: "In order to carry out a market transaction it is necessary to discover who it is that one wishes to deal with, to inform people that one wishes to deal and on what terms, to conduct negotiations leading up to a bargain, to draw up the contract, to undertake the inspection needed to make sure that the terms of the contract are being observed, and so on."[8] Dahlman crystallized the concept of transaction costs by describing them as "search and information costs, bargaining and decision costs, policing and enforcement costs."[9] Without the concept of transaction costs, which is largely absent from current economic theory, it is my contention that it is impossible to understand the working of the economic system, to analyze many of its problems in a useful way, or to have a basis for determining policy. The existence of trans-

8. See "The Problem of Social Cost," 114.
9. Carl J. Dahlman, "The Problem of Externality," *The Journal of Law and Economics* 22, no. 1 (April 1979): 148.

action costs will lead those who wish to trade to engage in practices which bring about a reduction of transaction costs whenever the loss suffered in other ways from the adoption of those practices is less than the transaction costs saved. The people one deals with, the type of contract entered into, the kind of product or service supplied, will all be affected. But perhaps the most important adaptation to the existence of transaction costs is the emergence of the firm. In my article on "The Nature of the Firm" I argued that, although production could be carried out in a completely decentralized way by means of contracts between individuals, the fact that it costs something to enter into these transactions means that firms will emerge to organize what would otherwise be market transactions whenever their costs were less than the costs of carrying out the transactions through the market. The limit to the size of the firm is set where its costs of organizing a transaction become equal to the cost of carrying it out through the market. This determines what the firm buys, produces, and sells. As the concept of transaction costs is not usually used by economists, it is not surprising that an approach which incorporates it will find some difficulty in getting itself accepted. We can best understand this attitude if we consider not the firm but the market.

III. The Market

Although economists claim to study the working of the market, in modern economic theory the market itself has an even more shadowy role than the firm. Alfred Marshall had a chapter "On Markets" in his *Principles of Economics,* but it was general in character and did not probe, perhaps because this was a topic reserved for what ultimately became *Industry and Trade.* In the modern textbook, the analysis deals with the determination of market prices, but discussion of the market itself has entirely disappeared. This is less strange than it seems. Markets are institutions that exist to facilitate exchange, that is, they exist in order to reduce the cost of carrying out exchange transactions. In an economic theory which assumes that transaction costs are nonexistent, markets have no function to perform, and it seems perfectly reasonable to develop the theory of exchange by an elaborate analysis of individuals exchanging nuts for apples on the edge of the forest or some similar fanciful example. This analysis certainly shows why there is a gain from trade, but it fails to deal with the factors which determine how much trade there is or what goods are traded. And when economists do speak of market structure, it has nothing to do with the market as an institution but refers to such things as the number of firms, product differentiation, and the like, the influence of the social institutions which facilitate exchange being completely ignored.

The provision of markets is an entrepreneurial activity and has a long history. In the medieval period in England, fairs and markets were organized by individuals under a franchise from the King. They not only provided the physical facilities for the fair or market but were also responsible for security (important in such unsettled times with a relatively weak government) and administered a court for settling disputes (the court of piepowder). Fairs and markets have continued to be provided in modern times, including exhibition halls and the like, and have often (again in England) been a municipal function. Of course, their relative importance has tended to diminish with the growth in the number of shops and similar facilities operated by private retailers and wholesalers. With the government providing security and with a more developed legal system, proprietors of the old markets no longer had to assume a responsibility for providing security or to undertake legal functions, although some courts of piepowder survived late into the nineteenth century.[10]

If the traditional markets of the past have diminished in importance, new markets have emerged in recent times of comparable importance in our modern economy. I refer to commodity exchanges and stock exchanges. These are normally organized by a group of traders (the members of the exchange)

10. For an account of the history of fairs and markets and the courts of piepowder, see Joseph G. Pease and Herbert Chitty, *Pease and Chitty's Law of Markets and Fairs,* 2nd ed. by Harold Parrish (London: C. Knight, 1958), 1–9, and Palgrave's *Dictionary of Political Economy* (London: Macmillan & Co., 1894–1901), S. V. "Fairs and Markets" and "Piepowder Court."

which owns (or rents) the physical facility within which transactions take place. All exchanges regulate in great detail the activities of those who trade in these markets (the times at which transactions can be made, what can be traded, the responsibilities of the parties, the terms of settlement, etc.), and they all provide machinery for the settlement of disputes and impose sanctions against those who infringe the rules of the exchange. It is not without significance that these exchanges, often used by economists as examples of a perfect market and perfect competition, are markets in which transactions are highly regulated (and this quite apart from any government regulation that there may be). It suggests, I think correctly, that for anything approaching perfect competition to exist, an intricate system of rules and regulations would normally be needed. Economists observing the regulations of the exchanges often assume that they represent an attempt to exercise monopoly power and aim to restrain competition. They ignore or, at any rate, fail to emphasize an alternative explanation for these regulations: that they exist in order to reduce transaction costs and therefore to increase the volume of trade. Adam Smith said this: "The interest of the dealers . . . in any particular branch of trade or manufactures, is always in some respects different from, and even opposite to, that of the publick. To widen the market and to narrow the competition, is always the interest of the dealers. To widen the market may frequently be agreeable enough to the interest of the publick; but to narrow the competition must always be against it . . ."[11] The eloquence and force of Adam Smith's denunciations of regulations designed to narrow the competition seem to have blinded us to the fact that dealers also have an interest in making regulations which widen the market, perhaps because this was a subject to which Adam Smith gave little attention. But there is, I believe, another reason for this neglect of the role which regulation may play in widening the market. Monopoly and impediments to trade such as tariffs are easily handled by normal

11. Adam Smith, *An Inquiry into the Nature and Causes of the Wealth of Nations,* vol. 1 of *The Glasgow Edition of the Works and Correspondence of Adam Smith,* ed. R. H. Campbell and A. S. Skinner, text ed. W. B. Todd (Oxford, 1976), 267.

price theory, whereas the absence of transaction costs in the theory makes the effect of a reduction in them difficult to incorporate in the analysis.

It is evident that, for their operation, markets such as those that exist today require more than the provision of physical facilities in which buying and selling can take place. They also require the establishment of legal rules governing the rights and duties of those carrying out transactions in these facilities. Such legal rules may be made by those who organize the markets, as is the case with most commodity exchanges. The main problems faced by the exchanges in this law making are the securing of the agreement of the members of the exchange and the enforcement of its rules. Agreement is facilitated in the case of commodity exchanges because the members meet in the same premises and deal in a restricted range of commodities; and enforcement of the rules is possible because the opportunity to trade on the exchange is itself of great value and the withholding of permission to trade is a sanction sufficiently severe to induce most traders to observe the rules of the exchange. When the physical facilities are scattered and owned by a vast number of people with very different interests, as is the case with retailing and wholesaling, the establishment and administration of a private legal system would be very difficult. Those operating in these markets have to depend, therefore, on the legal system of the State.[12]

IV. The Problem of Social Cost

The influence of the law on the working of the economic system is examined in "The Problem of Social Cost." The genesis of this paper throws some light on the present state of economic theory. In a previously published paper entitled "The Federal Communications Commission,"[13] I had argued that it would

12. For an analysis of organized futures markets which closely parallels mine and is certainly consistent with it, see Lester G. Telser and Harlow N. Higinbotham, "Organized Futures Markets: Costs and Benefits," *Journal of Political Economy* 85, no. 5 (1977): 969.

13. R. H. Coase, "The Federal Communications Commission," *The Journal of Law and Economics* (October 1959): 1–40.

be better if, in the United States, use of the various segments of the radio frequency spectrum was awarded to the highest bidders rather than coming about as a result of an administrative decree. But I did not leave the matter there. I went on to discuss what rights would be acquired by the successful bidder, a question which economists, thinking as they do of factors of production as physical units (tons of fertilizer, acres of land, etc.), usually take for granted. Lawyers, however, habitually think of what is bought and sold as consisting of a bundle of rights. It is easy to see why I was led to adopt the same approach in dealing with the radio frequency spectrum, since it is difficult to treat the use of the right to emit electrical radiations solely in physical terms, particularly since what can be achieved by emitting electrical radiations on a given frequency depends crucially on what use of this and adjacent frequencies is being made by others. It is impossible to think concretely about what would be paid for the use of a particular frequency unless there has been some specification of the rights possessed by all the people who use this and adjacent frequencies or who might use them. It was in this context that I developed the analysis first published in "The Federal Communications Commission" which I was subsequently to treat at much greater length in "The Problem of Social Cost." I was led to restate my argument in this more elaborate form because a number of economists, particularly at the University of Chicago, who had read the earlier article thought the analysis fallacious, and I hoped that I could overcome their doubts and objections by a fuller treatment.[14]

There is no difficulty in employing the same approach which I found useful in discussing the allocation of the radio frequency spectrum for the analysis of problems which economists are more accustomed to handle. Someone having the right to build a factory on a piece of land (and wishing to exercise that right) would normally also secure the right to prevent someone else from, say, planting wheat on it; and if operation of the factory

14. See Edmund W. Kitch, ed., "The Fire of Truth: A Remembrance of Law and Economics at Chicago, 1932–1970," *The Journal of Law and Economics* 26, no. 1 (April 1983): 220–22.

created noise or led to the emission of smoke, the factory-owner would wish to have the right to do this. The factory-owner would choose to use a particular site and create noise and emit smoke because this would produce a higher net income than alternative sites or modes of operation. Exercise of these rights would, of course, deny use of the land to agriculturalists and quiet and clean air to others.

If rights to perform certain actions can be bought and sold, they will tend to be acquired by those for whom they are most valuable either for production or enjoyment. In this process, rights will be acquired, subdivided, and combined, so as to allow those actions to be carried out which bring about that outcome which has the greatest value on the market. Exercise of the rights acquired by one person inevitably denies opportunities for production or enjoyment by others, for whom the price of acquiring the rights would be too high. Of course, in the process of acquisition, subdivision, and combination, the increase in the value of the outcome which a new constellation of rights allows has to be matched against the costs of carrying out the transactions needed to achieve that new constellation, and such a rearrangement of rights will only be undertaken if the cost of the transactions needed to achieve it is less than the increase in value which such a rearrangement makes possible.

What this approach makes clear is that there is no difference, analytically, between rights such as those to determine how a piece of land should be used and those, for example, which enable someone in a given location to emit smoke. Just as the possession of the right to build a factory on a piece of land normally gives the owner the right not to build on that site, so the right to emit smoke at a given site can be used to stop smoke being emitted from that site (by not exercising the right and not transferring it to someone else who will). How the rights will be used depends on who owns the rights and the contractual arrangements into which the owner has entered. If these arrangements are the result of market transactions, they will tend to lead to the rights being used in the way which is most valued, but only after deducting the costs involved in making these transactions. Transaction costs therefore play a crucial role in determining how rights will be used.

"The Problem of Social Cost," in which these views were presented in a systematic way, has been widely cited and discussed in the economics literature. But its influence on economic analysis has been less beneficial than I had hoped. The discussion has largely been devoted to sections III and IV of the article and even here has concentrated on the so-called "Coase Theorem," neglecting other aspects of the analysis. In sections III and IV, I examined what would happen in a world in which transaction costs were assumed to be zero. My aim in so doing was not to describe what life would be like in such a world but to provide a simple setting in which to develop the analysis and, what was even more important, to make clear the fundamental role which transaction costs do, and should, play in the fashioning of the institutions which make up the economic system. I examined two situations, one in which firms were liable to pay compensation for the harm which their actions imposed on others and one in which the firms were not liable. The example I used for illustrative purposes, one which had been used by my critics, was that of ranchers whose cattle strayed and destroyed the crops of neighbouring farmers. I showed, as I thought, that if transaction costs were assumed to be zero and the rights of the various parties well defined, the allocation of resources would be the same in both these situations. In my example, if the cattle-raiser had to pay to the crop-farmer the value of the damage caused by his cattle, he would obviously include this in his costs. But if the cattle-raiser were not liable for damage, the crop-farmer would be willing to pay (up to) the value of the damage to induce the cattle-raiser to stop it, so that for the cattle-raiser to continue his operations and bring about this crop damage would mean foregoing this sum, which would therefore become a cost of continuing to raise cattle. The damage imposes the same cost on the cattle-raiser in both situations. However, I also pointed out a factor which plays an important part in the subsequent argument but which does not always seem to have been noticed by my critics: that if the cattle-raiser were liable, it would

13

always be possible to negotiate abandonment of crop production or a change in the crop planted whenever this reduced the damage by an amount greater than the fall in the value of the crop (excluding damage). In addition, other measures may be taken to reduce damage, for example, fencing, when they cost less than the damage that they prevent. As a consequence, "the fall in the value of production elsewhere that would be taken into account in the costs of the cattle-raiser may well be less than the damage which the cattle would [otherwise] cause."[15] My conclusion was: ". . . the ultimate result (which maximizes the value of production) is independent of the legal system if the pricing system is assumed to work without cost."[16] This conclusion was formalized by Stigler as the "Coase Theorem," which he expressed as follows: ". . . under perfect competition private and social costs will be equal."[17]

A world without transaction costs has very peculiar properties. As Stigler has said of the "Coase Theorem": "The world of zero transaction costs turns out to be as strange as the physical world would be without friction. Monopolies would be compensated to act like competitors, and insurance companies would not exist."[18] I showed in "The Nature of the Firm" that, in the absence of transaction costs, there is no economic basis for the existence of the firm. What I showed in "The Problem of Social Cost" was that, in the absence of transaction costs, it does not matter what the law is, since people can always negotiate without cost to acquire, subdivide, and combine rights whenever this would increase the value of production. In such a world the institutions which make up the economic system have neither substance nor purpose. Cheung has even argued that, if transaction costs are zero, "the assumption of private property rights can be dropped without in

15. See "The Problem of Social Cost," 101.
16. See "The Problem of Social Cost," 104.
17. George J. Stigler, *The Theory of Price*, 3rd ed. (New York: Macmillan Co., 1966), 113.
18. George J. Stigler, "The Law and Economics of Public Policy: A Plea to the Scholars," *Journal of Legal Studies* 1 (1972): 12.

the least negating the Coase Theorem"[19] and he is no doubt right. Another consequence of the assumption of zero transaction costs, not usually noticed, is that, when there are no costs of making transactions, it costs nothing to speed them up, so that eternity can be experienced in a split second.

It would not seem worthwhile to spend much time investigating the properties of such a world. What my argument does suggest is the need to introduce positive transaction costs explicitly into economic analysis so that we can study the world that exists. This has not been the effect of my article. The extensive discussion in the journals has concentrated almost entirely on the "Coase Theorem," a proposition about the world of zero transaction costs. This response, although disappointing, is understandable. The world of zero transaction costs, to which the Coase Theorem applies, is the world of modern economic analysis, and economists therefore feel quite comfortable handling the intellectual problems it poses, remote from the real world though they may be. That much of the discussion has been critical of my argument is also quite understandable since, if I am right, current economic analysis is incapable of handling many of the problems to which it purports to give answers. A conclusion so depressing is hardly likely to be welcomed, and the resistance that my analysis has encountered is therefore quite natural. It is my view that the objections raised to the Coase Theorem and to my discussion of taxation schemes (the parts of my analysis in "The Problem of Social Cost" to which economists have given most attention) are invalid, unimportant, or irrelevant. In "Notes on the Problem of Social Cost," printed later in this volume, will be found the reasons why I think this is so. However, discussion of the Coase Theorem is concerned with a situation in which transaction costs, explicitly or implicitly, are assumed to be zero. It is in any case but a preliminary to the development of an analytical system capable of tackling the problems posed by the real world of positive transaction costs. However, it is my

19. Steven N. S. Cheung, *Will China Go 'Capitalist'?*, 2nd ed., Hobart Paper 94 (London: Institute of Economic Affairs, 1986), 37.

opinion that we will not be able to do this unless we first discard the approach at present used by most economists.

V. Marginal Cost Pricing

The support given to the proposal for marginal cost pricing, which I discussed in "The Marginal Cost Controversy," reprinted in this volume, provides an excellent illustration of the approach of modern economists. This support did not come from an obscure and little-regarded group of economists but from some of the most distinguished members of the economics profession. The originating article in the United States, which appeared in 1938, was written by Hotelling.[20] In England the most influential advocate of marginal cost pricing was Lerner, who published his analysis in 1944 but whose work dated from the 1930s.[21] During the war, Meade and Fleming, who were then in the economics section of the British Cabinet Office, wrote advocating marginal cost pricing in a symposium concerned with the problems of operating state enterprises. Keynes saw their paper and was so enthusiastic about it that he published it in the *Economic Journal,* of which he was editor.[22] Other economists have also advocated marginal cost pricing, but Hotelling, Lerner, Meade, Fleming, and Keynes make a formidable list.[23]

That the case for marginal cost pricing is persuasive goes without saying, since otherwise it could not have commended itself to so many able economists. Its logical basis is easily explained. The cost of the factors used in making a product is the value of what they would otherwise produce. Unless price

20. H. Hotelling, "The General Welfare in Relation to Problems of Taxation and of Railway and Utility Rates," *Econometrica* 6 (July 1938): 242–69.

21. A. Lerner, *The Economics of Control* (New York: Macmillan Co., 1944).

22. J. E. Meade and J. M. Fleming, "Price and Output Policy of State Enterprise," *Economic Journal* 54 (December 1944): 321–39.

23. See R. H. Coase, "The Theory of Public Utility Pricing and its Application," *The Bell Journal of Economics and Management Science* 1, no. 1 (Spring 1970): 113–23, for an account of the discussion of marginal cost pricing by these and other economists.

equals cost, consumers will not necessarily demand a product, even though its value to them is greater than that which the factors needed to make it would yield elsewhere. Since consumers have to decide not only what to consume but also how much, price should be equal to the cost of additional units of output, that is to say, marginal cost. As Samuelson has put it: "Only when prices of goods are equal to Marginal Costs is the economy squeezing from its scarce resources and limited technical knowledge the maximum of outputs. . . . Because Marginal Cost has this optimality property, it can with some care be used to detect inefficiency in any institutional setup."[24] This has suggested to many economists that all prices should be made equal to marginal cost.

A price equal to marginal cost would yield revenues sufficient to cover total costs if the average costs of the producer were rising with increases in output. Indeed, in these circumstances competition will normally ensure that marginal cost is equal to price without any need for government action. But if average costs are decreasing with increases in output and consequently marginal cost is less than average cost, a price equal to marginal cost will not raise enough revenue from consumers to cover total costs. To overcome this difficulty, it was proposed that the government should give a subsidy to the enterprise concerned equal to the amount by which receipts from consumers would fall short of total costs, the government raising the money required for the subsidy through taxation. It was the purpose of "The Marginal Cost Controversy" to point out the weaknesses of this policy.

Since there are innumerable products and services for which average costs would be decreasing with increases in output, and not all of them should be subsidized, the government would have to decide which of them should be supplied. The procedure which advocates of marginal cost pricing put forward to solve this problem was that the government (or those running the enterprises) should estimate how much consumers would be willing to pay to

24. Paul A. Samuelson, *Economics: An Introductory Analysis,* 6th ed. (New York: McGraw-Hill, 1964), 462.

obtain the quantity they would demand if price were equal to marginal cost, and if this showed that consumers would be willing to pay a sum which would cover total costs, the government would give the enterprise concerned the difference between total costs and receipts from consumers.

This seemed to me both an odd procedure and one which would lead to great inefficiency. It was odd in that, it having been decided that consumers would be willing to pay an amount which would cover total costs, they were not asked to do so. It would lead to inefficiency because, as consumers did not have to pay this amount, there would be very little information available upon which to base estimates of whether they would be willing to pay it. Furthermore, without a subsequent market test of whether the estimates were correct, those making them would do a less careful job (quite apart from the political factors that would come into play and would influence the government in deciding whether to subsidize a particular service). The proposal is a recipe for waste on a grand scale. The policy would also mean a redistribution of income in favour of consumers of goods produced in conditions of decreasing cost. Furthermore, the policy involves additional taxation, and this will tend to raise prices above marginal cost for those products or services which are the subject of taxation. The result would be that, in order to prevent prices being above marginal cost for some products, price is raised above marginal cost for others. The net gain from such a policy is not evident to me.

These were the points I emphasized in "The Marginal Cost Controversy." However, I have since come to realize the importance of a point which Tom Wilson made early on in the debate in the *Economic Journal*.[25] He drew attention to the close relationship between financial autonomy and the administrative structure. If there is a subsidy, the government will be concerned to keep down its amount and will therefore want to be involved, at least to some degree, in the administration of the subsidized service. Marginal cost pricing would therefore

25. Tom Wilson, "Price and Output Policy of State Enterprise: A Comment," *Economic Journal* 55 (1945): 254–61.

tend to lead to the substitution of state for private enterprise and of centralized for decentralized operations. The inefficiencies brought about by what will often be a very inappropriate administrative structure may well constitute the most serious disadvantage of marginal cost pricing. If efficiency is promoted by private enterprise and decentralized operations, financial autonomy is required. And financial autonomy is incompatible with marginal cost pricing.

Marginal cost pricing as a policy is largely without merit. How then can one explain the widespread support that it has enjoyed in the economics profession? I believe it is the result of economists using an approach which I have termed "blackboard economics." The policy under consideration is one which is implemented on the blackboard. All the information needed is assumed to be available and the teacher plays all the parts. He fixes prices, imposes taxes, and distributes subsidies (on the blackboard) to promote the general welfare. But there is no counterpart to the teacher within the real economic system. There is no one who is entrusted with the task that is performed on the blackboard. In the back of the teacher's mind (and sometimes in the front of it) there is, no doubt, the thought that in the real world the government would fill the role he plays. But there is no single entity within the government which regulates economic activity in detail, carefully adjusting what is done in one place to accord with what is done elsewhere. In real life we have many different firms and government agencies, each with its own interests, policies, and powers. The government implements its economic policy by setting up (or abolishing) a government agency, by changing the law in relation to liability or in some other way, by introducing a licensing arrangement, by giving authority over certain matters to the courts, by nationalizing (or denationalizing) an industry, and so on. What the government does is to choose among the social institutions which perform the functions of the economic system. Blackboard economics is undoubtedly an exercise requiring great intellectual ability, and it may have a role in developing the skills of an economist, but it misdirects our attention when thinking about economic policy. For this we need to consider the way in which the economic system would work with alternative institutional structures. And this requires a different approach from that used by most modern economists.

VI. The Pigovian Tradition and Modern Economic Analysis

Welfare economics—that part of economics which deals with, among other things, the role of government in regulating the working of the economic system—is to a very large extent based on the analysis in Pigou's *The Economics of Welfare,* first published in 1920, though it largely repeats arguments which appeared in his *Wealth and Welfare,* published in 1912.

In "The Problem of Social Cost," I said that Pigou's basic position was that, when defects were found in the working of the economic system, the way to put things right was through some form of governmental action. This view is expressed with numerous qualifications, but it represents the central tendency in his thought. Some have suggested that I was too harsh in my criticism of Pigou, but I believe what I said was essentially correct. I will demonstrate the character of Pigou's approach by examining a part of his work which I did not discuss in "The Problem of Social Cost," chapter 20 in part two of *The Economics of Welfare,* entitled "Intervention by Public Authorities."[26]

Pigou is concerned with the question of whether the national dividend might be increased by some kind of public intervention. He says: "In any industry, where there is reason to believe that the free play of self-interest will cause an amount of resources to be invested different from the amount that is required in the best interest of the national dividend, there is a *prima facie* case for public intervention."[27] He adds that this is, of course, only a *prima facie* case: "It is not sufficient to contrast the imperfect adjustments of unfettered private enterprise with the best adjustment that economists in their studies can imagine. For we cannot expect that any public authority will attain, or will even wholeheartedly seek, that ideal. Such

26. A. C. Pigou, *The Economics of Welfare,* 5th ed. (London: Macmillan & Co., 1952), 329–35.
27. Ibid., 331.

authorities are liable alike to ignorance, to sectional pressure and to personal corruption by private interest."[28]

However, Pigou argues that these defects of public intervention do not have the same force at all times and in all places. In England, and here he quotes Marshall, there is more honesty and unselfishness than there was, and the electorate is now able to check abuses of power and privilege. "This important fact implies that there is now a greater likelihood that any given piece of interference, by any given public authority, will prove beneficial than there was in former times."[29] He also notes that, as well as the "improvement in the working of existing forms of public authority, we have also to reckon with the invention of improved forms."[30] Municipal and similar representative bodies have four disadvantages so far as controlling or operating business is concerned: (1) they are primarily chosen for purposes other than that of intervention in industry; (2) their membership is constantly fluctuating; (3) their areas of operation are commonly determined by noncommercial considerations; and (4) they are subject to undesirable electoral pressure. However, according to Pigou, these "four disadvantages can be overcome . . . by the recently developed device of Commissions or *ad hoc* Boards. . . . The members of such Commissions can be specially chosen for their fitness for their task, their appointment can be for long periods, the area allotted to them can be suitably adjusted, and their terms of appointment can be such as to free them, in the main, from electoral pressure."[31] One example which he gives of such a Commission is the Interstate Commerce Commission. Pigou feels able to conclude: "The broad result is that modern developments in the structure and methods of governmental agencies have fitted these agencies for beneficial intervention in industry under conditions which would not have justified intervention in earlier times."[32] In this way, while making the point earlier in the chapter that we should not "contrast the

28. Ibid., 332.
29. Ibid., 333.
30. Ibid., 333.
31. Ibid., 334.
32. Ibid., 335.

imperfect adjustments of private enterprise with the best adjustment that economists in their studies can imagine," Pigou is able, by assuming the existence of (almost) perfectly functioning public bodies, in effect to do just that.

Pigou seems to have had no doubt that these Commissions would work in the way he describes. So, starting with a statement about the imperfections of government, Pigou discovers the perfect form of governmental organization and is therefore able to avoid enquiring into the circumstances in which the defects of public intervention would mean that such intervention would tend to make matters worse. Pigou's belief in the virtues of the independent regulatory commissions, which seem to us laughable today, was first expressed in *Wealth and Welfare* in 1912 and repeated in all editions of *The Economics of Welfare* without change. Pigou never seems to have thought it necessary to enquire whether his optimistic opinion about these commissions was justified by events in the subsequent forty years (the 1952 reprint is the last edition to contain new material). In all editions the Interstate Commerce Commission is referred to as the Interstate Railway Commission, and this body, created in 1887, is always described as "recently developed," which does not suggest any real interest in the subject.

All this shows very clearly the bent of Pigou's mind. Notwithstanding that Pigou was, as Austin Robinson observes, "primarily concerned . . . with 'fruit' rather than 'light'; with writing a theory of welfare that was applicable in practice," he did not make any detailed studies of the working of economic institutions. His discussion of any particular question seems to have been based on the reading of a few books or articles and often does not rise above the level of the secondary literature on which he relied. The examples to be found in his works are really illustrative of his position rather than the basis for it. Austin Robinson tells us that in his reading Pigou was "seeking always realistic illustrations for quotation in his own work," and this indicates his manner of working.[33] It is hardly

33. Austin Robinson, "Arthur Cecil Pigou," in the *International Encyclopedia of the Social Sciences*, vol. 12 (Macmillan Co. and Free Press, 1968), 92, 94. I possess Pigou's copy of Edward W. Bemis, *Municipal Monopolies*, 4th ed. (Thomas Y. Crowell & Co., 1904), cited on six occasions in chapters

surprising that, acquiring his illustrations in this way, Pigou often fails to realize their significance. For example, as I pointed out in "The Problem of Social Cost," the situation in which sparks from a railway locomotive could start fires which burnt woods on land adjoining the railway without the railway having to pay compensation to the owners of the woods (the legal position in England at the time Pigou was writing and one of which he had perhaps heard) had come about not because of a lack of governmental action but in consequence of it.

Modern economists use, in the main, the same approach as Pigou, although with some change in terminology and with an even greater detachment from the real world. Samuelson, in his *Foundations of Economic Analysis* (1947), summarizes, without dissent, Pigou's position as follows: ". . . his doctrine holds that the equilibrium of the closed economy under competition is correct except where there are technological external economies or diseconomies. Under these conditions, since each individual's actions have effects on others which he does not take into account in making his decisions, there is a *prima facie* case for intervention. But this holds only for technological factors (smoke nuisance etc) . . ."[34] The only difference in the more recent discussion is that the phrase "external economies or diseconomies" has been replaced by the word "externality," a term which appears to have been coined by Samuelson in the 1950s.[35] Thus, Hahn, writing in 1981, says that "we call an externality . . . an effect of one agent's actions on the wel-

20 ("Intervention by Public Authorities"), 21 ("Public Control of Monopoly"), and 22 ("Public Operation of Industry") in *The Economics of Welfare*. I will deposit this book in Special Collections, Regenstein Library, University of Chicago. A study of his markings and comments will indicate Pigou's manner of working.

34. Paul A. Samuelson, *Foundations of Economic Analysis* (Cambridge, Mass.: Harvard University Press, 1947), 208.

35. The earliest uses of the term "externality" that I have come across are contained in Samuelson's review of de Graaf's *Theoretical Welfare Economics* in the *Economic Journal* (September 1958): 539–41, and in his article, "Aspects of Public Expenditure Theories," *The Review of Economics and Statistics* (November 1958): 332–38. This article was a slight revision of a paper delivered in December, 1955.

fare of another." He adds that "ever since Marshall and Pigou it has been agreed that externalities constitute a *prima facie* case for government intervention in a market economy."[36] An externality is more usually defined as the effect of one person's decision on someone who is not a party to that decision. Thus, if A buys something from B, A's decision to buy affects B, but this effect is not considered to be an "externality." However, if A's transaction with B affects C, D, and E, who are not parties to the transaction, because, for example, it results in noise or smoke which impinge on C, D, and E, the effects on C, D, and E are termed "externalities." With this amendment, Hahn's statement embracing the Pigovian approach is representative of mainstream economic analysis. It should also be noted that when modern economists speak of governmental intervention, they usually seem to have in mind the imposition of taxes or, less frequently, direct regulation of the activities of the firms or individuals concerned.

This approach has serious weaknesses. It fails to disclose the factors which determine whether governmental intervention is desirable, and of what kind, and it ignores other possible courses of action. It has consequently misled economists in formulating their recommendations for economic policy. In particular, the existence of "externalities" does not imply that there is a *prima facie* case for governmental intervention, if by this statement is meant that, when we find "externalities," there is a presumption that governmental intervention (taxation or regulation) is called for rather than the other courses of action which could be taken (including inaction, the abandonment of earlier governmental action, or the facilitating of market transactions).

Assume that A, in manufacturing a product, emits smoke (which A has a right to do), harming C, with whom A has no contractual relations and of whose existence he may even be unaware. There is an "externality." Assume that the government is as able and well motivated as the Interstate Commerce

---

36. Frank Hahn, "Reflections on the Invisible Hand," *Lloyds Bank Review* (April 1982): 7–8. This article is reprinted in Frank Hahn, *Equilibrium and Macroeconomics* (Cambridge, Mass.: MIT Press, 1984), 111–33.

Commission of Pigou's imagination. What should it do? Consider the case in which the amount which C would pay to avoid the harm is less than the additional cost that would have to be borne by A to eliminate it. In these circumstances, the perfect government, anxious to maximize the national dividend, would do nothing, neither through taxation of A nor by direct regulation, to prevent the smoke emission. The "externality" would continue to exist and would not call for governmental intervention.

Now consider the case in which C would pay more to avoid the harm than the additional cost that would have to be incurred by A to eliminate it. We must first enquire why C has not made a bargain with A to end the emission of smoke, since a bargain would appear to be possible on terms which would be profitable to both A and C. The answer must be that the costs of making the transaction were such as to offset the gain that the transaction would bring. If this is the situation, what should this perfect government do? Just as A and C would take into account the costs of carrying out their transaction, so a perfect government would take into account its costs of discovering what C would pay to avoid the harm and the costs that A would have to incur in order to eliminate it, as well as the government's costs in administering whatever scheme is adopted. If the costs of investigation and administration are sufficiently high and/or the results obtained are sufficiently uncertain, with the consequence that the expected gains from governmental intervention are less than the costs involved, such a government would neither place a tax on A nor impose regulations which would eliminate the smoke. Another possibility would be to change the law to make A liable for the damage caused, which would make a transaction between A and C unnecessary. Still another would be to amend the legal requirements governing a contract between A and C so as to make this transaction less costly. But presumably this ideal government would already have taken into account the repercussions of such changes in the law on other transactions in other cases, and not having made them must have decided that the losses elsewhere would offset whatever benefit they might bring in this particular case. In the hypothetical example discussed in this paragraph, the costs of transacting and the costs involved in governmental action make it desirable that the "externality" should continue to exist and that no governmental intervention should be undertaken to eliminate it.

As we have seen, it is easy to show that the mere existence of "externalities" does not, of itself, provide any reason for governmental intervention. Indeed, the fact that there are transaction costs and that they are large[37] implies that many effects of people's actions will not be covered by market transactions. Consequently, "externalities" will be ubiquitous. The fact that governmental intervention also has its costs makes it very likely that most "externalities" should be allowed to continue if the value of production is to be maximized. This conclusion is strengthened if we assume that the government is not like Pigou's ideal but is more like his normal public authority—ignorant, subject to pressure, and corrupt. Whether there is a presumption, when we observe an "externality," that governmental intervention is desirable, depends on the cost conditions in the economy concerned. We can imagine cost conditions in which this presumption would be correct and also those in which it would not. It is wrong to claim that economic theory establishes such a presumption. What we are dealing with is a factual question. The ubiquitous nature of "externalities" suggests to me that there is a *prima facie* case against intervention, and the studies on the effects of regulation which have been made in recent years in the United States, ranging from agriculture to zoning, which indicate that regulation has commonly made matters worse, lend support to this view.

The concept of "externality" has come to play a central role in welfare economics, with results which have been wholly unfortunate. There are, without question, effects of their actions on others (and even on themselves) which people making decisions do not take into account. But, as employed today, the term carries with it the connotation that when "external-

37. See D. North and J. Wallis, "Measuring the Size of the Transaction Sector in the American Economy, 1870–1970," in *Long Term Factors in American Economic Growth,* edited by S. Engerman and R. Gallman, Studies on Income and Wealth, vol. 51 (National Bureau of Economic Research, 1987), 95–148.

ities" are found, steps should be taken by the government to eliminate them. As already indicated, the only reason individuals and private organizations do not eliminate them is that the gain from doing so would be offset by what would be lost (including the costs of making the arrangements necessary to bring about this result). If with governmental intervention the losses also exceed the gains from eliminating the "externality," it is obviously desirable that it should remain. To prevent it being thought that I shared the common view, I never used the word "externality" in "The Problem of Social Cost" but spoke of "harmful effects" without specifying whether decision-makers took them into account or not. Indeed, one of my aims in that article was to show that such "harmful effects" could be treated like any other factor of production, that it was sometimes desirable to eliminate them and sometimes not, and that it was unnecessary to use a concept such as "externality" in the analysis in order to obtain the correct result. However, I was clearly unsuccessful in cutting my argument loose from the dominant approach, since "The Problem of Social Cost" is often described, even by those sympathetic to my point of view, as a study of the problem of "externality."

It needs to be realized that, when economists study the working of the economic system, they are dealing with the effects of individuals' or organizations' actions on others operating within the system. That is our subject. If there were not such effects there would be no economic system to study. Individuals and organizations will, in furthering their own interests, take actions which facilitate or hinder what others want to do. They may supply labour services or withdraw them, provide capital equipment or decline to do so, emit smoke or prevent it, and so on. The aim of economic policy is to ensure that people, when deciding which course of action to take, choose that which brings about the best outcome for the system as a whole. As a first step, I have assumed that this is equivalent to maximizing the value of total production (and in this I am Pigovian).

Since, by and large, people choose to perform those actions which they think will promote their own interests, the way to alter their behaviour in the economic sphere is to make it in their interest to do so. The only means available to the government for doing this (apart from exhortation, which is commonly ineffective) is a change in the law or its administration. The forms such changes may take are many. They may amend the rights and duties which people are allowed to acquire or are deemed to possess, or they may make transactions more or less costly by altering the requirements for making a legally binding contract. Or they may change the penalties imposed by the courts when, outside contract, harm is inflicted on others. And, of course, the economists' favourite means, the attaching of taxes and subsidies to the performance of particular actions or governmental regulation prohibiting or requiring the performance of certain actions, may also be employed. Other changes in the way the legal system operates, such as changes of procedure in the courts, a redistribution of functions among government agencies, and (in the United States) a shift in the allocation of duties between the Federal Government and the States, will all affect the working of the economic system. Lawyers will no doubt find it easy to add to this list. Economic policy consists of choosing those legal rules, procedures, and administrative structures which will maximize the value of production. However, discovering the effects of varying the legal position on the working of the economic system is not easy, although progress is being made as a result of the researches of economists engaged in the new subject of "law and economics." I am hopeful that, as economists come to realize the unsatisfactory character of the current approach, the number of economists who will give their talents to this work will increase.

Economic policy involves a choice among alternative social institutions, and these are created by the law or are dependent on it. The majority of economists do not see the problem in this way. They paint a picture of an ideal economic system, and then, comparing it with what they observe (or think they observe), they prescribe what is necessary to reach this ideal state without much consideration for how this could be done. The analysis is carried out with great ingenuity but it floats in the air. It is, as I have phrased it, "blackboard economics." There is little investigation of how the economy actually operates, and in consequence it is hardly surprising that we find, as with Pigou, that the factual examples given are often quite misleading. A more recent case is that of Meade, who, in a much-cited article, uses the example of bees pollinating orchards as an interrelationship with which the market could not deal, obviously unaware of the contracts which are made between bee-keepers and orchard-owners, at least in the United States.[38]

A comprehensive illustration of the inadequacies of the usual approach of economists to questions of economic policy, at any rate in micro-economics, is provided by the example of the lighthouse, discussed in my article "The Lighthouse in Economics" reprinted in this volume. The lighthouse has been used by some of our greatest economists, from John Stuart Mill to Samuelson, as an example of a service which has to be provided by the government, and it has played a similar role in innumerable textbooks by lesser men. Yet none of these great economists who use the lighthouse example, so far as I am aware, has ever made a study of lighthouse finance and administration. In the circumstances it is hardly surprising that the statements they make on the subject are wrong, unclear, or misleading. Samuelson goes further than the older economists and, using an approach common among modern economists, argues not simply that no charge could be made for the services of a lighthouse (which is, as it happens, untrue) but that, even if it were possible to make a charge, this would

---

38. James E. Meade, "External Economies and Diseconomies in a Competitive Situation," *The Economic Journal* 62 (March 1952): 54–67. An interesting account of the institutional setting in which bee-keepers operate in the United States, including the contractual arrangements between bee-keepers and growers of crops, is to be found in David B. Johnson, "Meade, Bees and Externalities," *The Journal of Law and Economics* 16, no. 1 (April 1973): 35–52. A more detailed analysis of these contractual arrangements in which the effectiveness of the market is convincingly demonstrated is contained in Steven N. S. Cheung, "The Fable of the Bees: An Economic Investigation," in the same issue of *The Journal of Law and Economics*, 11–33. Meade furnishes another instance of the practice of economists of giving illustrations of their theoretical findings without feeling the need to investigate whether what they say corresponds to what is found in the real world.

be undesirable, since marginal cost is zero (the cost of an additional ship using the services of the lighthouse) and price should be equal to marginal cost. Samuelson does not proceed by comparing the results that would be achieved by a system in which there is a charge for lighthouse services with one in which the lighthouse service is financed out of general taxation. He starts with postulating the ideal situation (which he thinks is a zero price) and implies that this should be brought about, but without any consideration of what the effects of his policy would be on lighthouse operations. I argued that, in the case of England, in which there was a charge for lighthouse services, the lighthouse service was better adapted to the needs of shipowners with the existing system than it would be if it were financed out of general taxation. Whether or not my conclusion is sound is another matter. But it can only be disproved by making a comparison similar to the one I made and showing that I had not taken into account some relevant factors or had incorrectly evaluated the effects of some which had been considered. My conclusion cannot be refuted by demonstrating that what is achieved by my policy recommendation does not correspond to some ideal which is unattainable.

VII. The Way Ahead

I have suggested that economists need to adopt a new approach when considering economic policy. But a change in approach is not enough. Without some knowledge of what would be achieved with alternative institutional arrangements, it is impossible to choose sensibly among them. We therefore need a theoretical system capable of analyzing the effects of changes in these arrangements. To do this it is not necessary to abandon standard economic theory, but it does mean incorporating transaction costs into the analysis, since so much that happens in the economic system is designed either to reduce transaction costs or to make possible what their existence prevents. Not to include transaction costs impoverishes the theory. No doubt other factors should also be added. But it is not easy to improve the analysis without more knowledge than we now possess about how economic activities are actually carried out. The lighthouse example shows how far economists can go wrong if they are unaware of the facts. In my paper "Industrial Organization: A Proposal for Research," reprinted in this volume, I indicated how little we knew and how much there is to be discovered about the activities of firms and their contractual arrangements. Similarly, in "The Problem of Social Cost" I gave as examples of the kind of research required the need to study "the work of the broker in bringing parties together, the effectiveness of restrictive covenants, the problems of the large-scale real-estate development company, the operation of governmental zoning, and other regulating activities." Excellent work has been done since these papers were published but much remains to be done. The most daunting tasks that remain are those found in the new subject of "law and economics." The interrelationships between the economic system and the legal system are extremely complex, and many of the effects of changes in the law on the working of the economic system (the very stuff of economic policy) are still hidden from us. The essays in this book do little more than indicate the direction research should take. A long, arduous, but rewarding journey lies ahead.

TWO

The Nature of the Firm

Economic theory has suffered in the past from a failure to state clearly its assumptions. Economists in building up a theory have often omitted to examine the foundations on which it was erected. This examination is, however, essential not only to prevent the misunderstanding and needless controversy which arise from a lack of knowledge of the assumptions on which a theory is based, but also because of the extreme importance for economics of good judgment in choosing between rival sets of assumptions. For instance, it is suggested that the use of the word "firm" in economics may be different from the use of the term by the "plain man."[1] Since there is apparently a trend in economic theory towards starting analysis with the individual firm and not with the industry,[2] it is all the more necessary not only that a clear definition of the word "firm" should be given, but that its difference from a firm in the "real world," if it exists, should be made clear. Joan Robinson has said that "the two questions to be asked of a set of assumptions in economics are: Are they tractable? and: Do they correspond with the real world?"[3] Though, as Joan Robinson points out, "more often one set will be manageable and the other realistic," yet there may well be branches of theory where assumptions are both manageable and realistic. It is hoped to show in the

Reprinted from *Economica*, n.s., 4 (November 1937).

1. Joan Robinson, *Economics is a Serious Subject* (Cambridge, Eng.: W. Heffer & Sons, 1932), 12.

2. See Nicholas Kaldor, "The Equilibrium of the Firm," *Economic Journal* 44 (March 1934): 60–76.

3. Robinson, *Serious Subject*, 6.

following paper that a definition of a firm may be obtained which is not only realistic in that it corresponds to what is meant by a firm in the real world, but is tractable by two of the most powerful instruments of economic analysis developed by Marshall, the idea of the margin and that of substitution, together giving the idea of substitution at the margin.[4] Our definition must, of course, "relate to formal relations which are capable of being conceived exactly."[5]

I

It is convenient if, in searching for a definition of a firm, we first consider the economic system as it is normally treated by the economist. Let us consider the description of the economic system given by Sir Arthur Salter. "The normal economic system works itself. For its current operation it is under no central control, it needs no central survey. Over the whole range of human activity and human need, supply is adjusted to demand, and production to consumption, by a process that is automatic, elastic and responsive."[6] An economist thinks of the economic system as being co-ordinated by the price mechanism, and society becomes not an organization but an organism.[7] The economic system "works itself." This does not mean that there is no planning by individuals. These exercise foresight and choose between alternatives. This is necessarily so if there is to be order in the system. But this theory assumes that the direction of resources is dependent directly on the price mechanism. Indeed, it is often considered to be an objection to

4. J. M. Keynes, *Essays in Biography* (London: Macmillan & Co., 1933), 223–24.

5. L. Robbins, *Nature and Significance of Economic Science* (London: Macmillan & Co., 1932), 66.

6. This description is quoted with approval by D. H. Robertson, *The Control of Industry,* rev. ed. (London: Nisbet & Co., 1928), 85, and by Arnold Plant, "Trends in Business Administration," *Economica* 12, no. 35 (February 1932): 387. It appears in J. A. Salter, *Allied Shipping Control* (Oxford: Clarendon Press, 1921), 16–17.

7. See F. A. Hayek, "The Trend of Economic Thinking," *Economica* (May 1933).

economic planning that it merely tries to do what is already done by the price mechanism.[8] Sir Arthur Salter's description, however, gives a very incomplete picture of our economic system. Within a firm, the description does not fit at all. For instance, in economic theory we find that the allocation of factors of production between different uses is determined by the price mechanism. The price of factor A becomes higher in X than in Y. As a result, A moves from Y to X until the difference between the prices in X and Y, except in so far as it compensates for other differential advantages, disappears. Yet in the real world we find that there are many areas where this does not apply. If a workman moves from department Y to department X, he does not go because of a change in relative prices, but because he is ordered to do so. Those who object to economic planning on the grounds that the problem is solved by price movements can be answered by pointing out that there is planning within our economic system which is quite different from the individual planning mentioned above and which is akin to what is normally called economic planning. The example given above is typical of a large sphere in our modern economic system. Of course, this fact has not been ignored by economists. Marshall introduces organization as a fourth factor of production; J. B. Clark gives the co-ordinating function to the entrepreneur; Knight introduces managers who co-ordinate. As D. H. Robertson points out, we find "islands of conscious power in this ocean of unconscious co-operation like lumps of butter coagulating in a pail of buttermilk."[9] But in view of the fact that it is usually argued that co-ordination will be done by the price mechanism, why is such organization necessary? Why are there these "islands of conscious power"? Outside the firm, price movements direct production, which is co-ordinated through a series of exchange transactions on the market. Within a firm these market transactions are eliminated, and in place of the complicated market structure with exchange transactions is substituted the entrepreneur-co-ordinator, who

8. Ibid.
9. Robertson, *Control of Industry*, 85.

directs production.[10] It is clear that these are alternative methods of co-ordinating production. Yet, having regard to the fact that, if production is regulated by price movements, production could be carried on without any organization at all, well might we ask, Why is there any organization?

Of course, the degree to which the price mechanism is superseded varies greatly. In a department store, the allocation of the different sections to the various locations in the building may be done by the controlling authority or it may be the result of competitive price bidding for space. In the Lancashire cotton industry, a weaver can rent power and shop room and can obtain looms and yarn on credit.[11] This co-ordination of the various factors of production is, however, normally carried out without the intervention of the price mechanism. As is evident, the amount of "vertical" integration, involving as it does the supersession of the price mechanism, varies greatly from industry to industry and from firm to firm.

It can, I think, be assumed that the distinguishing mark of the firm is the supersession of the price mechanism. It is, of course, as Robbins points out, "related to an outside network of relative prices and costs,"[12] but it is important to discover the exact nature of this relationship. This distinction between the allocation of resources in a firm and the allocation in the economic system has been very vividly described by Maurice Dobb when discussing Adam Smith's conception of the capitalist: "It began to be seen that there was something more important than the relations inside each factory or unit captained by an undertaker; there were the relations of the undertaker with the rest of the economic world outside his immediate sphere . . . the undertaker busies himself with the division of labour inside each firm and he plans and organises consciously," but "he is related to the much larger economic

10. In the rest of this paper I shall use the term "entrepreneur" to refer to the person or persons who, in a competitive system, take the place of the price mechanism in the direction of resources.

11. United Kingdom, Parliament, Committee on Industry and Trade, *Survey of Textile Industries* 26 (1928).

12. Robbins, *Nature and Significance,* 71.

specialisation, of which he himself is merely one specialised unit. Here, he plays his part as a single cell in a larger organism, mainly unconscious of the wider role he fills."[13]

In view of the fact that, while economists treat the price mechanism as a co-ordinating instrument, they also admit the co-ordinating function of the "entrepreneur," it is surely important to enquire why co-ordination is the work of the price mechanism in one case and of the entrepreneur in another. The purpose of this paper is to bridge what appears to be a gap in economic theory between the assumption (made for some purposes) that resources are allocated by means of the price mechanism and the assumption (made for other purposes) that this allocation is dependent on the entrepreneur-co-ordinator. We have to explain the basis on which, in practice, this choice between alternatives is effected.[14]

II

Our task is to attempt to discover why a firm emerges at all in a specialized exchange economy. The price mechanism (considered purely from the side of the direction of resources) might be superseded if the relationship which replaced it was desired for its own sake. This would be the case, for example, if some people preferred to work under the direction of some other

---

13. Maurice Dobb, *Capitalist Enterprise and Social Progress* (London: G. Routledge & Sons, 1925), 20. Cf. also, H. D. Henderson, *Supply and Demand* (London: Nisbet & Co., 1932), 3–5.

14. It is easy to see when the State takes over the direction of an industry that, in planning it, it is doing something which was previously done by the price mechanism. What is usually not realized is that any business man, in organizing the relations among his departments, is also doing something which could be organized through the price mechanism. There is, therefore, point in Durbin's answer to those who emphasize the problems involved in economic planning that the same problems have to be solved by business men in the competitive system. (See E. F. M. Durbin, "Economic Calculus in a Planned Economy," *Economic Journal* 46 [December 1936]: 676–90.) The important difference between these two cases is that economic planning is imposed on industry, while firms arise voluntarily because they represent a more efficient method of organizing production. In a competitive system, there is an "optimum" amount of planning!

person. Such individuals would accept less in order to work under someone, and firms would arise naturally from this. But it would appear that this cannot be a very important reason, for it would rather seem that the opposite tendency is operating if one judges from the stress normally laid on the advantage of "being one's own master."[15] Of course, if the desire was not to be controlled but to control, to exercise power over others, then people might be willing to give up something in order to direct others; that is, they would be willing to pay others more than they could get under the price mechanism in order to be able to direct them. But this implies that those who direct pay in order to be able to do this and are not paid to direct, which is clearly not true in the majority of cases.[16] Firms might also exist if purchasers preferred commodities which are produced by firms to those not so produced; but even in spheres where one would expect such preferences (if they exist) to be of negligible importance, firms are to be found in the real world.[17] Therefore there must be other elements involved.

The main reason why it is profitable to establish a firm would seem to be that there is a cost of using the price mechanism. The most obvious cost of "organizing" production through the price mechanism is that of discovering what the relevant prices are.[18] This cost may be reduced but it will not be eliminated by the emergence of specialists who will sell this information. The costs of negotiating and concluding a separate contract for each exchange transaction which takes place on

15. Cf. Harry Dawes, "Labour Mobility in the Steel Industry," *Economic Journal* 44 (March 1934): 86, who instances "the trek to retail shopkeeping and insurance work by the better paid of skilled men due to the desire (often the main aim in life of a worker) to be independent."

16. Nonetheless, this is not altogether fanciful. Some small shopkeepers are said to earn less than their assistants.

17. G. F. Shove in "The Imperfection of the Market: a Further Note," *Economic Journal* 43 (March 1933): 116, n. 1, points out that such preferences may exist, although the example he gives is almost the reverse of the instance given in the text.

18. According to Nicholas Kaldor, "A Classificatory Note on the Deter-minateness of Equilibrium," *Review of Economic Studies* (February 1934): 123, it is one of the assumptions of static theory that "all the relevant prices . . . are known to all individuals." But this is clearly not true of the real world.

a market must also be taken into account.[19] Again, in certain markets, e.g., produce exchanges, a technique is devised for minimizing these contract costs; but they are not eliminated. It is true that contracts are not eliminated when there is a firm, but they are greatly reduced. A factor of production (or the owner thereof) does not have to make a series of contracts with the factors with whom he is co-operating within the firm, as would be necessary, of course, if this co-operation were a direct result of the working of the price mechanism. For this series of contracts is substituted one. At this stage, it is important to note the character of the contract into which a factor enters that is employed within a firm. The contract is one whereby the factor, for a certain remuneration (which may be fixed or fluctuating), agrees to obey the directions of an entrepreneur *within certain limits.*[20] The essence of the contract is that it should only state the limits to the powers of the entrepreneur. Within these limits, he can therefore direct the other factors of production.

There are, however, other disadvantages—or costs—of using the price mechanism. It may be desired to make a long-term contract for the supply of some article or service. This may be due to the fact that if one contract is made for a longer period instead of several shorter ones, then certain costs of making each contract will be avoided. Or, owing to the risk attitude of the people concerned, they may prefer to make a long- rather than a short-term contract. Now, owing to the difficulty of forecasting, the longer the period of the contract is for the supply of the commodity or service, the less possible and, indeed, the less desirable it is for the person purchasing

19. This influence was noted by Abbott Usher when discussing the development of capitalism. He says: "The successive buying and selling of partly finished products were sheer waste of energy." (*An Introduction to the Industrial History of England* [Boston: Houghton Mifflin Co., 1920], 13.) But he does not develop the idea nor consider why it is that buying and selling operations still exist.

20. It would be possible for no limits to the powers of the entrepreneur to be fixed. This would be voluntary slavery. According to Francis R. Batt, *The Law of Master and Servant,* 1st ed. (London: Sir I. Pitman & Sons, 1929), 18, such a contract would be void and unenforceable.

to specify what the other contracting party is expected to do. It may well be a matter of indifference to the person supplying the service or commodity which of several courses of action is taken, but not to the purchaser of that service or commodity. But the purchaser will not know which of these several courses he will want the supplier to take. Therefore, the service which is being provided is expressed in general terms, the exact details being left until a later date. All that is stated in the contract is the limits to what the person supplying the commodity or service is expected to do. The details of what the supplier is expected to do are not stated in the contract but are decided later by the purchaser. When the direction of resources (within the limits of the contract) becomes dependent on the buyer in this way, that relationship which I term a "firm" may be obtained.[21] A firm is likely, therefore, to emerge in those cases where a very short-term contract would be unsatisfactory. It is obviously of more importance in the case of services—labour—than it is in the case of the buying of commodities. In the case of commodities, the main items can be stated in advance and the details which will be decided later will be of minor significance.

We may sum up this section of the argument by saying that the operation of a market costs something and that, by forming an organization and allowing some authority (an "entrepreneur") to direct the resources, certain marketing costs are saved. The entrepreneur has to carry out his function at less cost, taking into account the fact that he may get factors of production at a lower price than the market transactions which he supersedes, because it is always possible to revert to the open market if he fails to do this.

The question of uncertainty is one which is often considered to be very relevant to the study of the equilibrium of the firm. It seems improbable that a firm would emerge without the existence of uncertainty. But those, for instance Knight,

21. Of course, it is not possible to draw a hard and fast line which determines whether there is a firm or not. There may be more or less direction. It is similar to the legal question of whether there is the relationship of master and servant or principal and agent. See the discussion of this problem below.

who make the *mode of payment* the distinguishing mark of the firm—fixed incomes being guaranteed to some of those engaged in production by a person who takes the residual, and fluctuating, income—would appear to be introducing a point which is irrelevant to the problem we are considering. One entrepreneur may sell his services to another for a certain sum of money, while the payment to his employees may be mainly or wholly a share in profits.[22] The significant question would appear to be why the allocation of resources is not done directly by the price mechanism.

Another factor that should be noted is that exchange transactions on a market and the same transactions organized within a firm are often treated differently by governments or other bodies with regulatory powers. If we consider the operation of a sales tax, it is clear that it is a tax on market transactions and not on the same transactions organized within the firm. Now since these are alternative methods of "organization"— by the price mechanism or by the entrepreneur—such a regulation would bring into existence firms which otherwise would have no raison d'être. It would furnish a reason for the emergence of a firm in a specialized exchange economy. Of course, to the extent that firms already exist, such a measure as a sales tax would merely tend to make them larger than they would otherwise be. Similarly, quota schemes, and methods of price control which imply that there is rationing and which do not apply to firms producing such products for themselves, by allowing advantages to those who organize within the firm and not through the market, necessarily encourage the growth of firms. But it is difficult to believe that it is measures such as those mentioned in this paragraph which have brought firms into existence. Such measures would, however, tend to have this result if they did not exist for other reasons.

These, then, are the reasons why organizations such as firms exist in a specialized exchange economy in which it is generally assumed that the distribution of resources is "organized" by the price mechanism. A firm, therefore, consists

22. The views of Knight are examined below in more detail.

of the system of relationships which comes into existence when the direction of resources is dependent on an entrepreneur.

The approach which has just been sketched would appear to offer an advantage, in that it is possible to give a scientific meaning to what is meant by saying that a firm gets larger or smaller. A firm becomes larger as additional transactions (which could be exchange transactions co-ordinated through the price mechanism) are organized by the entrepreneur, and it becomes smaller as he abandons the organization of such transactions. The question which arises is whether it is possible to study the forces which determine the size of the firm. Why does the entrepreneur not organize one less transaction or one more? It is interesting to note that Knight considers that

> the relation between efficiency and size is one of the most serious problems of theory, being, in contrast with the relation for a plant, largely a matter of personality and historical accident rather than of intelligible general principles. But the question is peculiarly vital because the possibility of monopoly gain offers a powerful incentive to *continuous and unlimited* expansion of the firm, which force must be offset by some equally powerful one making for decreased efficiency (in the production of money income) with growth in size, if even boundary competition is to exist.[23]

Knight would appear to consider that it is impossible to treat scientifically the determinants of the size of the firm. On the basis of the concept of the firm developed above, this task will now be attempted.

It was suggested that the introduction of the firm was due primarily to the existence of marketing costs. A pertinent question to ask would appear to be (quite apart from the monopoly considerations raised by Knight), Why, if by organizing one can eliminate certain costs and in fact reduce the cost of pro-

---

23. Frank H. Knight, *Risk, Uncertainty and Profit*, Preface to the Reissue (London: London School of Economics and Political Science, 1933).

duction, are there any market transactions at all?[24] Why is not all production carried on by one big firm? There would appear to be certain possible explanations.

First, as a firm gets larger, there may be decreasing returns to the entrepreneur function, that is, the costs of organizing additional transactions within the firm may rise.[25] Naturally, a point must be reached where the costs of organizing an extra transaction within the firm are equal to the costs involved in carrying out the transaction in the open market or to the costs of organizing by another entrepreneur. Second, it may be that, as the transactions which are organized increase, the entrepreneur fails to place the factors of production in the uses where their value is greatest, that is, fails to make the best use of the factors of production. Again, a point must be reached where the loss through the waste of resources is equal to the marketing costs of the exchange transaction in the open market or to the loss if the transaction was organized by another entrepreneur. Finally, the supply price of one or more of the factors of production may rise, because the "other advantages" of a small firm are greater than those of a large firm.[26] Of course, the

24. There are certain marketing costs which could only be eliminated by the abolition of "consumers' choice" and these are the costs of retailing. It is conceivable that these costs might be so high that people would be willing to accept rations because the extra product obtained was worth the loss of their choice.

25. This argument assumes that exchange transactions on a market can be considered as homogeneous, which is clearly untrue in fact. This complication is taken into account below.

26. For a discussion of the variation of the supply price of factors of production to firms of varying size, see E. A. G. Robinson, *The Structure of Competitive Industry* (London: Nisbet & Co., 1931). It is sometimes said that the supply price of organizing ability increases as the size of the firm increases because men prefer to be the heads of small independent businesses rather than the heads of departments in a large business. See Eliot Jones, *The Trust Problem in the United States* (New York: Macmillan Co., 1921), 231, and D. H. Macgregor, *Industrial Combination* (London: G. Bell & Sons, 1906), 63. This is a common argument of those who advocate Rationalization. It is said that larger units would be more efficient, but owing to the individualistic spirit of the smaller entrepreneurs, they prefer to remain independent, apparently in spite of the higher income which their increased efficiency under Rationalization makes possible.

actual point where the expansion of the firm ceases might be determined by a combination of the factors mentioned above. The first two reasons given most probably correspond to the economists' phrase of "diminishing returns to management."[27]

The point has been made in the previous paragraph that a firm will tend to expand until the costs of organizing an extra transaction within the firm become equal to the costs of carrying out the same transaction by means of an exchange on the open market or the costs of organizing in another firm. But if the firm stops its expansion at a point below the costs of marketing in the open market and at a point equal to the costs of organizing in another firm, in most cases (excluding the case of "combination")[28] this will imply that there is a market transaction between these two producers, each of whom could organize it at less than the actual marketing costs. How is the paradox to be resolved? If we consider an example, the reason for this will become clear. Suppose A is buying a product from B and that both A and B could organize this market transaction at less than its present cost. B, we can assume, is not organizing one process or stage of production, but several. If A therefore wishes to avoid a market transaction, he will have to take over all the processes of production controlled by B. Unless A takes over all the processes of production, a market transaction will still remain, although it is a different product that is bought. But we have previously assumed that as each producer expands he becomes less efficient; the additional costs of organizing extra transactions increase. It is probable that A's cost of organizing the transactions previously organized by B will be greater than B's cost of doing the same thing. A, therefore, will take over the whole of B's organization only if his cost of organizing B's work is not greater than B's cost by an amount equal to the costs of carrying out an exchange transaction on the open market. But once it becomes economical to have a

27. This discussion is, of course, brief and incomplete. For a more thorough discussion of this particular problem, see Kaldor, "Equilibrium of the Firm," and Austin Robinson, "The Problem of Management and the Size of Firms," *Economic Journal* 44 (June 1934): 242–57.

28. A definition of this term is given below.

market transaction, it also pays to divide production in such a way that the cost of organizing an extra transaction in each firm is the same.

Up to now it has been assumed that the exchange transactions which take place through the price mechanism are homogeneous. In fact, nothing could be more diverse than the actual transactions which take place in our modern world. This would seem to imply that the costs of carrying out exchange transactions through the price mechanism will vary considerably, as will the costs of organizing these transactions within the firm. It seems therefore possible that, quite apart from the question of diminishing returns, the costs of organizing certain transactions within the firm may be greater than the costs of carrying out the exchange transactions in the open market. This would necessarily imply that there were exchange transactions carried out through the price mechanism; but would it mean that there would have to be more than one firm? Clearly not, for all those areas in the economic system where the direction of resources was not dependent directly on the price mechanism could be organized within one firm. The factors which were discussed earlier would seem to be the important ones, though it is difficult to say whether "diminishing returns to management" or the rising supply price of factors is likely to be the more important.

Other things being equal, therefore, a firm will tend to be larger:

(a) the less the costs of organizing and the slower these costs rise with an increase in the transactions organized;

(b) the less likely the entrepreneur is to make mistakes and the smaller the increase in mistakes with an increase in the transactions organized;

(c) the greater the lowering (or the less the rise) in the supply price of factors of production to firms of larger size.

Apart from variations in the supply price of factors of production to firms of different sizes, it would appear that the costs of organizing and the losses through mistakes will increase with an increase in the spatial distribution of the transactions organized, in the dissimilarity of the transactions, and in the probability of changes in the relevant prices.[29] As more transactions are organized by an entrepreneur, it would appear that the transactions would tend to be either different in kind or different in place. This furnishes an additional reason why efficiency will tend to decrease as the firm gets larger. Inventions which tend to bring factors of production nearer together, by lessening spatial distribution, tend to increase the size of the firm.[30] Changes like the telephone and the telegraph, which tend to reduce the cost of organizing spatially, will tend to increase the size of the firm. All changes which improve managerial technique will tend to increase the size of the firm.[31]

It should be noted that the definition given above of a firm can be used to give more precise meanings to the terms "com-

29. This aspect of the problem is emphasized by Kaldor, "Equilibrium of the Firm." Its importance in this connection had been previously noted by E. A. G. Robinson, *Competitive Industry,* 83–106. This assumes that an increase in the probability of price movements increases the costs of organizing within a firm more than it increases the cost of carrying out an exchange transaction on the market—which is probable.

30. This would appear to be the importance of the treatment of the technical unit by E. A. G. Robinson, *Competitive Industry*, 27–33. The larger the technical unit, the greater the concentration of factors, and therefore the firm is likely to be larger.

31. It should be noted that most inventions will change both the costs of organizing and the costs of using the price mechanism. In such cases, whether the invention tends to make firms larger or smaller will depend on the relative effect on these two sets of costs. For instance, if the telephone reduces the costs of using the price mechanism more than it reduces the costs of organizing, then it will have the effect of reducing the size of the firm.

An illustration of these dynamic forces is furnished by Maurice Dobb, *Russian Economic Development Since the Revolution* (New York: E. P. Dutton & Co., 1928), 68: "With the passing of bonded labour the factory, as an establishment where work was organised under the whip of an overseer, lost its *raison d'être* until this was restored to it with the introduction of power machinery after 1846." It seems important to realize that the passage from the domestic system to the factory system is not a mere historical accident, but is conditioned by economic forces. This is shown by the fact that it is possible to move from the factory system to the domestic system, as in the Russian example, as well as vice versa. It is the essence of serfdom that the price mechanism is not allowed to operate. Therefore, there has to be direction from some organizer. When, however, serfdom passed, the price mechanism was allowed to operate. It was not until machinery drew workers into one locality that it paid to supersede the price mechanism and the firm again emerged.

bination" and "integration."[32] There is a combination when transactions which were previously organized by two or more entrepreneurs become organized by one. This becomes integration when it involves the organization of transactions which were previously carried out among the entrepreneurs on a market. A firm can expand in either or both of these two ways. The whole of the "structure of competitive industry" becomes tractable by the ordinary technique of economic analysis.

III

The problem which has been investigated in the previous section has not been entirely neglected by economists, and it is now necessary to consider why the reasons given above for the emergence of a firm in a specialized exchange economy are to be preferred to the other explanations which have been offered.

It is sometimes said that the reason for the existence of a firm is to be found in the division of labour. This is the view of Usher, a view which has been adopted and expanded by Maurice Dobb. The firm becomes "the result of an increasing complexity of the division of labour. . . . The growth of this economic differentiation creates the need for some integrating force without which differentiation would collapse into chaos; and it is as the integrating force in a differentiated economy that industrial forms are chiefly significant."[33] The answer to this argument is an obvious one. The "integrating force in a differentiated economy" already exists in the form of the price mechanism. It is perhaps the main achievement of economic science that it has shown there is no reason to suppose that specialization must lead to chaos.[34] The reason given by Maurice Dobb is therefore inadmissible. What has to be explained

32. This is often called "vertical integration," combination being termed "lateral integration."

33. Dobb, *Capitalist Enterprise and Social Progress*, 10. Usher's views are to be found in his *Industrial History of England*, 1–18.

34. Cf. J. B. Clark, *The Distribution of Wealth* (New York: Macmillan Co., 1931), 19, who speaks of the theory of exchange as being the "theory of the organization of industrial society."

is why one integrating force (the entrepreneur) should be sub-stituted for another integrating force (the price mechanism).

The most interesting reasons (and probably the most widely accepted) which have been given to explain this fact are those to be found in Knight's *Risk, Uncertainty and Profit.* His views will be examined in some detail.

Knight starts with a system in which there is no uncertainty:

> Acting as individuals under absolute freedom but with-out collusion men are supposed to have organised eco-nomic life with the primary and secondary division of labour, the use of capital, etc., developed to the point familiar in present-day America. The principal fact which calls for the exercise of the imagination is the internal organisation of the productive groups or es-tablishments. With uncertainty entirely absent, every individual being in possession of perfect knowledge of the situation, there would be no occasion for anything of the nature of responsible management or control of productive activity. Even marketing transactions in any realistic sense would not be found. The flow of raw materials and productive services to the consumer would be entirely automatic.[35]

Knight says that we can imagine this adjustment as being "the result of a long process of experimentation worked out by trial-and-error methods alone," while it is not necessary "to imagine every worker doing exactly the right thing at the right time in a sort of 'pre-established harmony' with the work of others. There might be managers, superintendants, etc., for the purpose of co-ordinating the activities of individuals," though these managers would be performing a purely routine function, "without responsibility of any sort."[36]

Knight then continues:

> With the introduction of uncertainty—the fact of ig-norance and the necessity of acting upon opinion rather

---

35. Knight, *Risk, Uncertainty and Profit,* 267.
36. Ibid., 267–68.

than knowledge—into this Eden-like situation, its character is entirely changed. . . . With uncertainty present doing things, the actual execution of activity, becomes in a real sense a secondary part of life; the primary problem or function is deciding what to do and how to do it.[37]

This fact of uncertainty brings about the two most important characteristics of social organization:

In the first place, goods are produced for a market, on the basis of entirely impersonal prediction of wants, not for the satisfaction of the wants of the producers themselves. The producer takes the responsibility of forecasting the consumers' wants. In the second place, the work of forecasting and at the same time a large part of the technological direction and control of production are still further concentrated upon a very narrow class of the producers, and we meet with a new economic functionary, the entrepreneur. . . . When uncertainty is present and the task of deciding what to do and how to do it takes the ascendancy over that of execution the internal organisation of the productive groups is no longer a matter of indifference or a mechanical detail. Centralisation of this deciding and controlling function is imperative, a process of "cephalisation" . . . is inevitable . . .[38]

The most fundamental change is

the system under which the confident and venturesome assume the risk or insure the doubtful and timid by guaranteeing to the latter a specified income in return for an assignment of the actual results. . . . With human nature as we know it it would be impracticable or very unusual for one man to guarantee to another a definite result of the latter's actions without being given power to direct his work. And on the other hand

37. Ibid., 268.
38. Ibid., 268–295.

the second party would not place himself under the direction of the first without such a guarantee. . . . The result of this manifold specialisation of function is the enterprise and wage system of industry. Its existence in the world is the direct result of the fact of uncertainty.[39]

These quotations give the essence of Knight's theory. The fact of uncertainty means that people have to forecast future wants. Therefore, you get a special class springing up who directs the activities of others to whom it gives guaranteed wages. It acts because good judgment is generally associated with confidence in one's judgment.[40]

Knight would appear to leave himself open to criticism on several grounds. First of all, as he himself points out, the fact that certain people have better judgment or better knowledge does not mean that they can only get an income from it by themselves actively taking part in production. They can sell advice or knowledge. Every business buys the services of a host of advisers. We can imagine a system where all advice or knowledge was bought as required. Again, it is possible to get a reward from better knowledge or judgment not by actively taking part in production but by making contracts with people who are producing. A merchant buying for future delivery represents an example of this. But this merely illustrates the point that it is quite possible to give a guaranteed reward providing that certain acts are performed without directing the performance of those acts. Knight says: "With human nature as we know it it would be impracticable or very unusual for one man to guarantee to another a definite result of the latter's actions without being given power to direct his work." This is surely incorrect. A large proportion of jobs is done to contract, that is, the contractor is guaranteed a certain sum providing he performs certain acts. But this does not involve any direction. It does mean, however, that the system of relative prices has been changed and that there will be a new arrangement of the

39. Ibid., 270.
40. Ibid., 269–70.

factors of production.[41] The fact that Knight mentions that the "second party would not place himself under the direction of the first without such a guarantee" is irrelevant to the problem we are considering. Finally, it seems important to notice that, even in the case of an economic system where there is no uncertainty, Knight considers that there would be co-ordinators, though they would perform only a routine function. He immediately adds that they would be "without responsibility of any sort," which raises the question, By whom are they paid and why? It seems that nowhere does Knight give a reason why the price mechanism should be superseded.

IV

It would seem important to examine one further point, and that is the relevance of this discussion to the general question of the "cost curve of the firm."

It has sometimes been assumed that a firm is limited in size under perfect competition if its cost curve slopes upward,[42] while under imperfect competition it is limited in size because it will not pay to produce more than the output at which marginal cost is equal to marginal revenue.[43] But it is clear that a firm may produce more than one product; therefore, there appears to be no *prima facie* reason why this upward slope of the cost curve in the case of perfect competition or the fact that marginal cost will not always be below marginal revenue in the case of imperfect competition should limit the size of the firm.[44] Joan Robinson makes the simplifying assumption

41. This shows that it is possible to have a private enterprise system without the existence of firms. Though, in practice, the two functions of enterprise (which actually influences the system of relative prices by forecasting wants and acting in accordance with such forecasts) and management (which accepts the system of relative prices as being given) are normally carried out by the same persons, yet it seems important to keep them separate in theory. This point is further discussed below.

42. See Kaldor, "Equilibrium of the Firm," and Robinson, "Problem of Management."

43. Austin Robinson calls this the "Imperfect Competition" solution for the survival of the small firm.

44. Austin Robinson's conclusion in "Problem of Management," 249, n. 1, would appear to be definitely wrong. He is followed by Horace J. White, Jr.,

that only one product is being produced.[45] But it is clearly important to investigate how the number of products produced by a firm is determined, while no theory which assumes that only one product is in fact produced can have very great practical significance.

It might be replied that under perfect competition, since everything that is produced can be sold at the prevailing price, there is no need for any other product to be produced. But this argument ignores the fact that there may be a point where it is less costly to organize the exchange transactions of a new product than to organize further exchange transactions of the old product. This point can be illustrated in the following way. Imagine, following von Thunen, that there is a town, the consuming centre, and that industries are located around this central point in rings. These conditions are illustrated in the following diagram in which *A, B,* and *C* represent different industries.

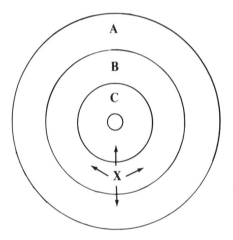

"Monopolistic and Perfect Competition," *American Economic Review* (December 1936): 645, n. 27. Mr. White states: "It is obvious that the size of the firm is limited in conditions of monopolistic competition."

45. Joan Robinson, *The Economics of Imperfect Competition* (London: Macmillan & Co., 1933), 17.

Imagine an entrepreneur who starts controlling exchange transactions from X. Now as he extends his activities in the same product (B), the cost of organizing increases until at some point it becomes equal to that of a dissimilar product which is nearer. As the firm expands, it will therefore from this point include more than one product (A and C). This treatment of the problem is obviously incomplete,[46] but it is necessary to show that merely proving that the cost curve turns upwards does not give a limitation to the size of the firm. So far we have only considered the case of perfect competition; the case of imperfect competition would appear to be obvious.

To determine the size of the firm, we have to consider the marketing costs (that is, the costs of using the price mechanism) and the costs of organizing of different entrepreneurs, and then we can determine how many products will be produced by each firm and how much of each it will produce. It would therefore appear that Shove[47] in his article on "Imperfect Competition" was asking questions which Joan Robinson's cost-curve apparatus cannot answer. The factors mentioned above would seem to be the relevant ones.

V

Only one task now remains: and that is, to see whether the concept of a firm which has been developed fits in with that existing in the real world. We can best approach the question of what constitutes a firm in practice by considering the legal relationship normally called that of "master and servant" or "employer and employee."[48] The essentials of this relationship have been given as follows:

46. As has been shown above, location is only one of the factors influencing the cost of organizing.

47. Shove, "Imperfection of the Market," 115. In connection with an increase in demand in the suburbs and the effect of the price charged by suppliers, Shove asks: ". . . why do not the old firms open branches in the suburbs?" If the argument in the text is correct, this is a question which Joan Robinson's apparatus cannot answer.

48. The legal concept of "employer and employee" and the economic concept of a firm are not identical, in that the firm may imply control over another person's property as well as over their labour. But the identities of

(1) The servant must be under the duty of rendering personal services to the master or to others on behalf of the master, otherwise the contract is a contract for sale of goods or the like.

(2) The master must have the right to control the servant's work, either personally or by another servant or agent. It is this right of control or interference, of being entitled to tell the servant when to work (within the hours of service) and when not to work, and what work to do and how to do it (within the terms of such service) which is the dominant characteristic in this relation and marks off the servant from an independent contractor, or from one employed merely to give to his employer the fruits of his labour. In the latter case, the contractor or performer is not under the employer's control in doing the work or effecting the service; he has to shape and manage his work so as to give the result he has contracted to effect.[49]

We thus see that it is the fact of direction which is the essence of the legal concept of "employer and employee," just as it was in the economic concept which was developed above. It is interesting to note that Batt says further:

That which distinguishes an agent from a servant is not the absence or presence of a fixed wage or the payment only of commission on business done, but rather the freedom with which an agent may carry out his employment.[50]

We can therefore conclude that the definition we have given is one which closely approximates the firm as it is considered in the real world.

Our definition is therefore realistic. Is it manageable? This ought to be clear. When we are considering how large a firm

---

these two concepts are sufficiently close for an examination of the legal concept to be of value in appraising the worth of the economic concept.

49. Batt, *Master and Servant*, 6.
50. Ibid., 7.

will be, the principle of marginalism works smoothly. The question always is, Will it pay to bring an extra exchange transaction under the organizing authority? At the margin, the costs of organizing within the firm will be equal either to the costs of organizing in another firm or to the costs involved in leaving the transaction to be "organized" by the price mechanism. Business men will be constantly experimenting, controlling more or less, and in this way equilibrium will be maintained. This gives the position of equilibrium for static analysis. But it is clear that the dynamic factors are also of considerable importance, and an investigation of the effect changes have on the cost of organizing within the firm and on marketing costs generally will enable one to explain why firms get larger and smaller. We thus have a theory of moving equilibrium. The above analysis would also appear to have clarified the relationship between initiative and enterprise and management. Initiative means forecasting and operates through the price mechanism by the making of new contracts. Management proper merely reacts to price changes, rearranging the factors of production under its control. That the business man normally combines both functions is an obvious result of the marketing costs which were discussed above. Finally, this analysis enables us to state more exactly what is meant by the "marginal product" of the entrepreneur. But an elaboration of this point would take us far from our comparatively simple task of definition and clarification.

THREE

Industrial Organization: A Proposal for Research

It is somewhat of an embarrassment to present a paper on the subject of industrial organization at a meeting sponsored by the National Bureau to celebrate its fifty years of service to the economics profession and to the public at large. That the National Bureau has had an extraordinary—and beneficial—impact on our thinking and work in many areas of economics is something which cannot be disputed. But, and this is the source of my embarrassment, the National Bureau has carried out very little research directly concerned with problems of industrial organization. I should find it difficult to know how to proceed with this paper, were it not that I believe that, in the future, the National Bureau ought to conduct much more research in the field of industrial organization. Indeed, it is just the kind of research which the National Bureau handles in so masterly a fashion: the careful collection of detailed information and its assembly to reveal the patterns of economic behaviour, which seems to me essential if ever we are to make progress in understanding the forces which determine the organization of industry. So, if I have very little to say about the work of the National Bureau in the past, I am hopeful that what I (and others) have to say on this occasion will result in the National Bureau's conducting such an extensive program of research that those of you who are fortunate enough to

Reprinted from *Policy Issues and Research Opportunities in Industrial Organization,* edited by Victor R. Fuchs, vol. 3 of *Economic Research: Retrospective and Prospect,* NBER General Series, no. 96 (Cambridge: National Bureau of Economic Research, 1972), 59–73. ©1972 by The National Bureau of Economic Research, Inc. All rights reserved.

attend the centenary celebrations will hear the National Bureau praised by the speakers for its achievements in the field, not of business cycles, but of industrial organization.

This neglect of industrial organization by the National Bureau is not a peculiarity of its own. It is, in large part, a reflection of what has been happening in economic research generally. Very little work is done on the subject of industrial organization at the present time, as I see the subject, since what is commonly dealt with under this heading tells us almost nothing about the organization of industry. You may remember the occasion on which Sherlock Holmes drew the Inspector's attention to the "curious incident of the dog in the nighttime." This brought the comment from the Inspector: "The dog did nothing in the nighttime." Holmes then remarked: "That was the curious incident."[1] I could not help recalling this conversation when contemplating the present state of the subject of industrial organization.

What is curious about the treatment of the problems of industrial organization in economics is that it does not now exist. We all know what is meant by the organization of industry. It describes the way in which the activities undertaken within the economic system are divided up among firms. As we know, some firms embrace many different activities; while for others the range is narrowly circumscribed. Some firms are large; others, small. Some firms are vertically integrated; others are not. This is the organization of industry or—as it used to be called—the structure of industry. What one would expect to learn from a study of industrial organization would be how industry is organized now, and how this differs from what it was in earlier periods; what forces were operative in bringing about this organization of industry, and how these forces have been changing over time; what the effects would be of proposals to change, through legal action of various kinds, the

---

1. In the version as originally published I said that this exchange was between Holmes and Dr. Watson. It was in fact between Holmes and Inspector Gregory (in the "Adventure of Silver Blaze"). I am indebted to S. C. Littlechild, who drew my attention to this inexcusable blunder which I have now corrected.

forms of industrial organization. Such a subject, solidly buttressed by the kind of research the National Bureau does so well, would enable us to appraise the worth of actions, and proposals for action, which have as their aim a modification of the way in which industry is organized.

This description of the organization of industry, which reflects the traditional view of the subject, is, however, almost certainly too narrow a conception of its scope. Firms are not the only organizations which undertake economic activities. Apart from associations of various sorts and nonprofit organizations (which may, however, be regarded as special kinds of firm), there is also a large number of governmental agencies which undertake economic activities, many of them of great importance. Almost all, if not indeed all, of these economic activities of government—whether it be police protection, garbage collection, the provision of utility services, education, or hospitals—are also provided by firms (or other analogous institutions). It should surely be part of the task of studies on industrial organization to describe the economic activities which are performed by governmental agencies, and to explain why the carrying out of these economic activities is divided up among private organizations and governments in the way that it is.[2]

Let us now look at how the subject is treated today. I will take as examples two of the most respected books on the subject: Stigler's *The Organization of Industry* and Bain's *Industrial Organization*. Stigler has this to say in his first chapter: "Let us start this volume on a higher plane of candor than it will always maintain: there is no such subject as industrial organization. The courses taught under this heading have for their purpose the understanding of the structure and behavior of the industries (goods and service producers) of an economy. These courses deal with the size structure of firms (one or many, 'concentrated' or not), the causes (above all the economies of scale) of this size structure, the effects of concentra-

---

2. I should like to refer here to an unpublished paper by Victor Fuchs, "Some Notes Toward a Theory of the Organization of Production," which examines this question and makes clear its significance.

tion on competition, the effects of competition upon prices, investment, innovation, and so on. But this is precisely the content of economic theory—price or resource allocation theory, now often given the unfelicitous name of microeconomics." As to why there are industrial organization courses in addition to those on economic theory, Stigler gives two reasons. The first is that theory courses are very formal in character and cannot go into studies of the empirical measurement of cost curves, concentration, and so forth. The second is that theory courses cannot go into public policy questions, particularly antitrust and regulation; and, as Stigler phrases it, "the course on industrial organization takes on these chores."[3]

Bain tells us that his book's general subject is "the organization and operation of the enterprise sector of a capitalist economy." He describes his approach as "external and behavioristic." He is concerned with "the environmental settings within which enterprises operate and in how they behave in their settings as producers, sellers and buyers." He gives "major emphasis to the relative incidence of competitive and monopolistic tendencies in various industries or markets."[4] What Bain produces is essentially a special sort of price theory book, dealing with such questions as the effects of concentration and the significance of these supposed effects for antitrust policy. Bain suggests that an interest in what the firm does (its internal operations) is in some sense related to management science, and he seems to link this with teaching how businesses ought to be run,[5] although it seems to me that the question could be studied without any such aim in mind. Bain's view of the subject (although not, of course, the way he handles it) is not essentially different from that of Stigler. Essentially, both Stigler and Bain consider the subject of industrial organization as applied price theory. Caves, in his book *American Industry: Structure, Conduct, Performance,* is even more explicit: "The

3. George J. Stigler, *The Organization of Industry* (Homewood, Ill.: Richard D. Irwin, 1968), 1.

4. See Joe S. Bain, *Industrial Organization* (New York: John Wiley and Sons, 1968), vii.

5. Ibid.

subject of 'industrial organization' applies the economist's models of price theory to the industries in the world around us.''[6]

Industrial organization has become the study of the pricing and output policies of firms, especially in oligopolistic situations (often called a study of market structure, although it has nothing to do with how markets function). It has not helped, of course, that there is no theory of oligopoly or, what comes to the same thing, that there are too many theories of oligopoly. But beyond this problem—and I do not intend to suggest that the questions tacked are unimportant—it is clear that modern economists writing on industrial organization have taken a very narrow view of the scope of their subject.

Now, this was not always the case. If you go to a library, you will find shelves of books written in the 1920s and 1930s dealing in detail with the organization of particular industries. And there was a good deal of more general literature (particularly in the United States) dealing with the problems of what was termed integration, both horizontal and vertical. For example, there was the study published in 1924 by Willard Thorp, *The Integration of Industrial Operations*. And in the Cambridge Economics Series in England, there were such general books as D. H. Robertson's *The Control of Industry* (1928) and E. A. G. Robinson's *The Structure of Competitive Industry* (1931). Earlier, of course, there had been Alfred Marshall's *Industry and Trade* (1919) (from which many British treatments took their inspiration). These works varied greatly in their range and treatment, from the discussion of workers' councils by Robertson to the historical account of industrial development by Marshall; from the casual empiricism of the English writers to the detailed statistical investigations of Willard Thorp. But they were all characterized by an interest in how industry was organized, in all its richness and complexity.

It was certainly works such as these which gave me my view of the subject of industrial organization. But what was

6. See Richard Caves, *American Industry: Structure, Conduct, Performance* (Englewood Cliffs, N.J.: Prentice-Hall, 1967), 14.

lacking in the literature, or so I thought, was a theory which would enable us to analyze the determinants of the organization of industry. It was this situation which led me to write, in the early 1930s, my paper "The Nature of the Firm"[7]—an article much cited and little used. This nonuse is not altogether surprising, since the problems that the theory was intended to illuminate have not been of much interest to economists in recent years. But if we are to tackle the problems of industrial organization seriously, a theory is needed.

What determines what a firm does? To answer this question, it is necessary to understand why a firm exists at all, since this gives us a clue as to the direction in which to look in order to uncover what determines what a firm does. In my day as a student (and perhaps this is still true today), the pricing system was presented as an automatic self-regulating system. In Sir Arthur Salter's words: "The normal economic system works itself." The allocation of resources was co-ordinated by the pricing system. Put as simply as this, it seemed to me then, and it still does, that this description does not fit at all what happens within the firm. A workman does not move from Department Y to Department X because the price in X has risen enough relative to the price in Y to make the move worthwhile for him. He moves from Y to X because he is ordered to do so.

As D. H. Robertson picturesquely put it, we find "islands of conscious power in this ocean of unconscious co-operation like lumps of butter coagulating in a pail of buttermilk." Outside the firm, price determines the allocation of resources, and their use is co-ordinated through a series of exchange transactions on the market. Within the firm, these market transactions are eliminated, and the allocation of resources becomes the result of an administrative decision. Why does the firm assume the burden of the costs of establishing and running this administrative structure, when the allocation of resources could be left to the pricing system? The main reason is that there are costs that have to be incurred in using the market, and these costs

7. See "The Nature of the Firm," 33–55.

can be avoided by the use of an administrative structure. If transactions are carried out through the market, there are the costs of discovering what the relevant prices are; there are the costs of negotiating and completing a separate contract for each market transaction; and there are other costs besides. Of course, the firm is attached to the market, and all contracting is not eliminated. But the owner of a factor of production does not have to make a series of contracts with the owners of the other factors of production with whom he is co-operating within the firm.

The source of the gain from having a firm is that the operation of a market costs something and that, by forming an organization and allowing the allocation of resources to be determined administratively, these costs are saved. But, of course, the firm has to carry out its task at a lower cost than the cost of carrying out the market transactions it supersedes, because it is always possible to revert to the market if the firm fails to do so. And, of course, for the individual firm, the alternative is some other firm which can take over the task if its costs are lower.

The way in which industry is organized is thus dependent on the relation between the costs of carrying out transactions on the market and the costs of organizing the same operations within that firm which can perform this task at the lowest cost. Furthermore, the costs of organizing an activity within any given firm depend on what other activities the firm is engaged in. A given set of activities will facilitate the carrying out of some activities but hinder the performance of others. It is these relationships which determine the actual organization of industry. But having said this, how far ahead are we? We know very little about the cost of conducting transactions on the market or what they depend on; we know next to nothing about the effects on costs of different groupings of activities within firms. About all we know is that the working out of these interrelationships leads to a situation in which viable organizations are small in relation to the economic system of which they are a part.

We are, in fact, appallingly ignorant about the forces which determine the organization of industry. We do, it is true, have some idea of why it is that an increase in the activities organized within the firm tends to produce strains within the administrative structure which raise the costs of organizing additional operations (even if similar to those already undertaken): the rise in cost occurs both because the administrative costs themselves rise, and because those making decisions make more mistakes and fail to allocate resources wisely. This is, more or less, the conventional treatment of the management problem in economics.[8] But as firms expand their functions, it seems to me that they are likely to embrace activities which are more widely scattered geographically, and which are, in other ways, more diverse in character. This, I think, must play its part in limiting the expansion of the firm. This is, in fact, a special case of the effects on costs of the combining of different activities within a single firm—not all of which will be adverse. But the existence of such interrelationships suggests that an efficient distribution of activities among firms would involve particular (and different) groupings of activities within the firms (which is, indeed, what we observe). We would not expect firms to be similar in the range of activities that they embrace; but, so far as I am aware, the distribution of activities among firms is not something on which we have much to say.

Why is it that we seem to have so little to say? In part, it can be explained by the character of the economic analysis which apparently deals with the organization of industry—by which I mean the treatment of the optimum size of the firm and of economies of scale. This analysis, which sounds as if it is dealing with the organization of industry (although it does not), tends to reassure those who might be worried by a more conspicuous gap. It is not difficult to see what is wrong with the theory of the optimum size of the firm as presented in economics. First of all, what is wanted is not a statement about *the* optimum size of the firm (presumably with a different optimum for each industry), but a theory which concerns itself with the optimum distribution of activities, or functions, among

8. See Oliver E. Williamson, "Internal Organization and Limits to Firm Size," in *Corporate Control and Business Behavior* (Englewood Cliffs, N.J.: Prentice-Hall, 1970), 14–40.

firms. Second, the theory of the optimum size of the firm is not about the size of the firm, in the sense of dealing with the activities carried out by the firm, but is concerned with the determination of the size of its output. Moreover, even here current theory is only concerned with the output of particular products, or a generalized product, and not with the range of products produced by the firm. This last statement is somewhat overbold, since economists may also use value or assets or number of employees to measure the size of the firm—but I am, at any rate, correct in saying that there is very little discussion about what firms actually do.

The discussion of economies of scale is largely concerned with the relation of costs to output (the derivation, in effect, of the cost schedule). Such discussion tells us nothing about the effect on costs of conducting one activity, of undertaking another activity, or about the relative costs to different kinds of firms of undertaking particular activities. Still less does it deal with the extent to which there is "contracting out" as the output of a product (or generalized product) is increased. What has happened is that the character of the analysis in which economists have engaged has not seemed to demand an answer to the question I have been raising.

I would not, however, wish to omit mention of the one paper which does attempt to deal with these questions, namely, Stigler's article "The Division of Labor is Limited by the Extent of the Market."[9] As we all know, this statement of Adam Smith, although correct (all of Adam Smith's statements are correct), has caused some perplexity, since it did not seem to be consistent with the existence of competitive conditions. In the course of resolving this problem, Stigler discusses the conditions which lead to the emergence of specialized firms and which influence the extent of vertical integration. Stigler does not take us very far, but he takes us as far as we have gone.

I have said that the character of the analysis used by economists has tended to conceal the fact that certain problems in industrial organization are not being tackled. But I think there

9. See Stigler, *Organization of Industry,* 129–41.

is a much more important reason for this neglect: interest in industrial organization has tended to be associated with the study of monopoly, the control of monopoly, and antitrust policy. This is not a recent development. In the late nineteenth century, when economists came to be interested in problems of industrial organization, they were confronted with the problem of the trust in the United States and the cartel in Germany. It was therefore natural that, with the development of antitrust policy in the United States, interest in the antitrust aspects of industrial organization came to dominate the subject.

This has had its good and its bad effects but, in my opinion, the bad by far outweigh the good. It has, no doubt, raised the morale of many scholars working on problems of industrial organization because they feel that they are engaged on work which has important policy implications. It has had the salutary result of focusing these scholars' attention on real problems concerning the way in which the economic system operates. It has also led them to utilize some sources of information which might otherwise have been neglected. Still, in other respects the effects seem to me to have been unfortunate. The desire to be of service to one's fellows is, no doubt, a noble motive, but it is not possible to influence policy if you do not give an answer. It has therefore encouraged men to become economic statesmen—men, that is, who provide answers even when there are no answers. This tendency has discouraged a critical questioning of the data and of the worth of the analysis, leading the many able scholars in this field to tolerate standards of evidence and analysis which, I believe, they would otherwise have rejected. This association with policy—and antitrust policy in particular—gave a direction to the study of industrial organization which prevented certain questions from being raised or, at any rate, made it more difficult for them to be raised. The facts as stated in antitrust cases were accepted as correct (or substantially so). The ways in which the problem was viewed by the lawyers (judges and advocates) were accepted as the ways in which we should approach the problem. The opinions of the judges often became the starting point of the analysis, and an attempt was made to make sense of what they had said. This so tangled the discussion that most economists were apparently unaware of having failed. It is true that this is beginning to change as a result of the work of, among others, Adelman and McGee,[10] but the dominant approach is still, I think, as I have stated it.

One important result of this preoccupation with the monopoly problem is that if an economist finds something—a business practice of one sort or other—that he does not understand, he looks for a monopoly explanation. And as we are very ignorant in this field, the number of ununderstandable practices tends to be rather large, and the reliance on a monopoly explanation is frequent. More recently, the desire to reduce the burden of taxes has become another way of explaining why businesses adopt the practices they do. In fact, the situation is such that if we ever achieved a system of limited government (and, therefore, low taxation) and the economic system were clearly seen to be competitive, we would have no explanation at all for the way in which the activities performed in the economic system are divided among firms. We would be unable to explain why General Motors was not a dominant factor in the coal industry, or why A & P did not manufacture airplanes.

May I give an illustration taken from a recent article in *The Journal of Law and Economics?* The article is by John L. Peterman, "The Clorox Case and the Television Rate Structures."[11] Procter and Gamble acquired Clorox and the merger was challenged under the antitrust laws. A large part of the case against Procter and Gamble was that they were able to obtain discounts for television advertising of the order of twenty-five to thirty per cent—discounts which were not available to smaller firms. This led many to the conclusion that it was a manifestation of monopoly in the television industry and an example of price discrimination. However, a careful study by Peterman showed that the discount structure was, in fact, designed to compensate for the fact that those who purchased

10. See, for example, Morris A. Adelman, "The A and P Case: A Study in Applied Economic Theory," *Quarterly Journal of Economics* 63 (May 1949): 238–57, and John S. McGee, "Predatory Price Cutting: The Standard Oil (N.J.) Case," *The Journal of Law and Economics* (October 1958): 137–69.

11. John L. Peterman, "The Clorox Case and the Television Rate Structures," *The Journal of Law and Economics* 11 (October 1968): 321–422.

advertising time in the same way as Procter and Gamble obtained, on the average, worse time (time with a smaller audience). In fact, if the amounts paid were related not to time but to audience size, the advantages which Procter and Gamble were alleged to have, disappeared.

This is, I think, a common situation. There is some unusual feature—in this case, large discounts. The conclusion is immediately drawn: monopoly. What people do not normally do is inquire whether it may not be the case that the practice in question is a necessary element in bringing about a competitive situation. If this were done, I suspect that a good deal of supposed monopoly would disappear, and competitive conditions would be seen to be more common than is now generally believed. In similar fashion, vertical integration (let us say, a manufacturer acquiring retail outlets) is often thought of as a foreclosure, a means of keeping out other manufactures, rather than as a possibly more efficient method of distribution. Similarly, mergers tend to be thought of as methods of obtaining monopoly, or they are related to the business cycle, and the possibility that they may bring economies, although not ignored, tends to receive less attention.

I have given instances of the way in which the association of the study of industrial organization with antitrust policy has created a disposition to search for monopolistic explanations for all business practices whose justification is not obvious to the meanest intelligence. But surely, you will ask, economists have not confined themselves to the role of camp followers to the judges and the antitrust lawyers in the Department of Justice and the Federal Trade Commission? The answer is that they have not so confined themselves—but it is questionable whether what they have done has been more useful. During the last twenty years, a major preoccupation of economists working in what is called industrial organization has been the study of concentration in particular industries and its effects. The effects they looked for were monopolistic, and the way they expected them to be manifested was in higher profits. As it seems to me (and I must confess that this is not a field with which I have great familiarity), the results obtained flattered only to deceive. There was a relationship between concentration and profitability, weak it is true, but, we are told, statistically significant. On theoretical grounds, it was rather puzzling. If the elasticity of supply to the industry was high, or the elasticity of demand for its products was high, one would not expect any relation between concentration and profitability. And if fewness of producers is supposed to bring greater profits as a result of collusion, there are many factors other than fewness of numbers which affect the likelihood of successful collusion. So it was rather strange that there was any detectable relationship at all. There were other puzzling features of the results, such as that the relationship became worse the more sharply defined the industry. But perhaps we should cease worrying about the significance of these concentration studies. I say this because of an article entitled "The Antitrust Task Force Deconcentration Recommendation" which has recently appeared. (It is a critique of a proposal which took the conclusion of these studies seriously and tried to do something about it.)[12] The author, Yale Brozen, claims that the results achieved in these concentration studies reflect disequilibrium conditions in the periods in which the studies were made. If the calculations are reworked for later periods, high profit rates tend to decline, low rates tend to rise. If the results reported by Brozen hold up after the criticism to which they inevitably (and rightly) will be exposed, there can, I think, be little doubt that this article brings an era to an end. The study of concentration and its effects will be in shambles. Should this really turn out to be the position, the present may well be a good time to pick up the pieces and start again.[13] That some rethinking of our theory is called for seems to me clear. But just as important, at the present stage, would be the gathering in a systematic way of new data on the organization of industry so that we can be better aware of what it is that we must explain.

12. Yale Brozen, "The Antitrust Task Force Deconcentration Recommendation," *The Journal of Law and Economics* 13 (October 1970): 279–92.

13. It has been suggested to me that the lack of any significant relationship between concentration and profitability does not imply that there may be a significant relationship between concentration and other aspects of industrial organization. This may well be true. However, I doubt whether we will understand the reasons for these relationships until we make a direct attack on the problem.

I should now like to return to the undertaking of economic activities by organizations other than firms and, particularly, by governmental organizations. Somewhat surprisingly, this is not a subject with which economists have been much concerned. Insofar as they have considered this topic, it was as part of a discussion of what the government *ought* to do, whether by taxation, regulation, or operation, to improve the working of the economic system; of these three policies, the least attention has been given to government operation. In any case, the discussion had two weaknesses. First, no serious investigation was made of how the policies advocated would work out in practice. To justify government action, it was enough to show that the "market"—or perhaps more accurately, private enterprise—failed to achieve the optimum. That the results of the government action proposed might also fall short of the optimum was little explored, and in consequence the conclusions reached have little value for appraising public policy.

The discussion, however, has a further weakness which is more relevant to my main theme here. It seems to have been implicitly assumed that the same considerations which led welfare economists to see the need for government action would also motivate those whose active support was required to bring about the political changes necessary to implement these policy recommendations. In this we are wiser than we were, in large part because of the new "economic theory of politics." We are beginning to perceive the nature of the forces which bring about changes in the law—and there is no necessary relationship between the strength of forces favouring such changes and the gain from such changes as seen by economists. It suggests that economists interested in promoting particular economic policies should investigate the framework of our political system to discover what modifications are required if their economic policies are to be adopted and should count in the cost of these political changes. This presupposes that the relationship between the character of the political institutions and the adoption of a particular economic policy—in our case, government operation of industry—has been discovered. We do not know much about these relationships, but uncovering them seems to ⁓⁓ ⁓ ⁓⁓⁻ ⁺⁻⁾ be assumed by students of industrial organization.

It is easy to observe that the extent of government participation in industry has varied over time, has varied among industries, and has varied over geographical areas. I have no doubt that, as a result of research on this aspect of industrial organization, the factors which have contributed to these differences will be uncovered. It is my hope that the National Bureau will participate in this work.

I have suggested that what is wanted is a large-scale systematic study of the organization of industry in the United States. I have also suggested that this would yield best results if conducted in an atmosphere in which the scientific spirit is not contaminated by a desire (or felt obligation) to find quick solutions to difficult policy issues. Where else could such conditions of scientific purity be found than in the National Bureau? This proposal for more research is founded on my belief that it is unlikely that we shall see significant advances in our theory of the organization of industry until we know more about what it is that we must explain. An inspired theoretician might do as well without such empirical work, but my own feeling is that the inspiration is most likely to come through the stimulus provided by the patterns, puzzles, and anomalies revealed by the systematic gathering of data, particularly when the prime need is to break our existing habits of thought.

I said that the National Bureau has done very little in the field of industrial organization. But the subject has not been completely ignored and, as Stigler has indicated (no doubt correctly), there is much to be learnt about industrial organization in National Bureau studies on finance, taxation, and technological advances.[14] But there are works sponsored by the National Bureau which deal squarely with industrial organization, and I should say something about them. That they are works of high scholarship, dealing with topics of great importance, is not in dispute; but with the present state of the discipline, it is hardly surprising that these works should have ignored or touched only lightly upon certain issues, or that the treatment was in other respects incomplete.

14. See George J. Stigler, Foreword to *Diversification and Integration in American Industry,* by Michael Gort (New York: National Bureau of Economic Research, 1962), xxi.

The chief works published by the National Bureau on industrial organization would seem to be: Solomon Fabricant, *The Trend of Government Activity in the United States since 1900* (1952); Ralph L. Nelson, *Merger Movements in American Industry* (1959); and Michael Gort, *Diversification and Integration in American Industry* (1962).

I will first say something about Fabricant's work, since it deals with government activity, an aspect of industrial organization which seems to me to have been somewhat neglected. This book does not confine itself to questions of public finance or regulation, which is important, revealing as it does an interest on the part of the National Bureau in the role of government as an organizer of economic activity. The discussion is, however, largely concerned with analyzing the composition of government employment and expenditures, with relating these to the totals for the economy as a whole, with discovering trends in the aggregates, and with similar questions. Of itself, the study does not throw much light on the factors which cause the government to operate economic enterprises, but it does provide a good deal of data which would be useful in an investigation which had this as its aim. I would hope that in some future study the National Bureau will collect detailed information about government operations in such a form that, as a result of analysis, we will discover the factors which cause government operation to be chosen against other methods of economic organization. In this connection I would hope that the National Bureau makes a study of government contracting, since the question at issue is not simply one of government versus private enterprise but also of government operation versus "contracting out" for products and services which the government itself demands.

Next, let us consider the books of Nelson and Gort, which deal with problems of industrial organization of a more traditional kind. Nelson's impressive work is mainly concerned with the development of time series for mergers in the United States; with relating merger movements to business cycles; and with testing, insofar as his data allow, the main explanations advanced to account for the variations in merger activity. Nelson does not give many details of the kind of organization created

72

by the mergers (the kind of activities that were brought together within the same organization), nor does he deal with what happened after the merger was consummated. As a consequence, we are not able to judge what the role of the various merger movements was in shaping the industrial structure of the United States, or how far they were a response to fundamental changes which required such modifications in organization to promote efficiency. All this, I may add, is recognized by Nelson, who concludes: "The important and interesting job of producing answers remains to be done."[15]

Of the three works that I have mentioned, that by Gort comes closest to what I have in mind when I speak of the research on industrial organizations that we need today. Gort does deal with the question of the range of activities organized within the firm, and there can be few problems of importance in industrial organization on which he does not touch. However, Gort abandoned the more straightforward methods of earlier investigators, such as Willard Thorp. He makes the central theme of his book a study of diversification. He measures trends in diversification and seeks to discover the economic characteristics of diversifying firms and of the industries entered by diversifying firms. Degrees of diversification are not, however, easy to define or to measure, and the results which Gort presents are difficult to interpret without knowledge of the underlying industrial structure. An approach to the organization of industry via a study of diversification is not without interest, but it presents a strange first step. It is as if we started an investigation of eating habits by measuring the degree of diversification in the foods consumed by each individual, rather than by discovering what the patterns of food consumption actually are.

In my view, what is wanted in industrial organization is a direct approach to the problem. This would concentrate on what activities firms undertake, and it would endeavor to discover the characteristics of the groupings of activities within

15. See Ralph L. Nelson, *Merger Movements in American Industry* (New York: National Bureau of Economic Research, 1959), 126.

73

firms. Which activities tend to be associated and which do not? The answer may well differ for different kinds of firm; for example, for firms of different size, or for those with a different corporate structure, or for firms in different industries. It is not possible to forecast what will prove to be of importance before such an investigation is carried out; which is, of course, why it is needed. In addition to studying what happens within firms, studies should also be made of the contractual arrangements between firms (long-term contracts, leasing, licensing arrangements of various kinds including franchising, and so on), since market arrangements are the alternative to organization within the firm. The study of mergers should be extended so that it becomes an integral part of the main subject. In addition to a study of the effects on the rearrangement of functions among firms through mergers, we also ought to take into account "dismergers" (the breaking up of firms); the transfer of departments or divisions between firms; the taking on of new activities and the abandonment of old activities; and also—something which tends to be forgotten—the emergence of new firms.

Studies such as those I have just outlined would bring under review the whole of the organization of industry in the United States, and they would put us in a position to start the long and difficult task of discovering what the forces are which shape it. It is my hope that the National Bureau will play a major role in bringing about this renaissance in the study of industrial organization.

FOUR

The Marginal Cost Controversy

I. The State of the Debate

I wish to discuss in this article the question of how prices ought to be determined in conditions of decreasing average costs. In particular, I wish to discuss one answer to this question which is by now familiar to most economists and which may be summarized as follows:

(a) The amount paid for each unit of the product (the price) should be made equal to marginal cost

(b) Since, when average costs are decreasing, marginal costs are less than average costs, the total amount paid for the product will fall short of total costs

(c) The amount by which total costs exceed total receipts (the loss, as it is sometimes termed) should be a charge on the government and should be borne out of taxation

This view has been supported by H. Hotelling,[1] A. P. Lerner,[2] J. E. Meade, and J. M. Fleming.[3] It has aroused consid-

Reprinted from *Economica*, n.s., 13 (August 1946).

1. H. Hotelling, "The General Welfare in Relation to Problems of Taxation and of Railway and Utility Rates," *Econometrica* 6, no. 3 (July 1938): 242–69.

2. A. P. Lerner, *The Economics of Control* (New York: Macmillan Co., 1944). Lerner had earlier set out this view in articles in the *Review of Economic Studies* and in the *Economic Journal*.

3. J. E. Meade and J. M. Fleming, "Price and Output Policy of State Enterprise," *Economic Journal* 54 (December 1944): 321–39. See also J. E. Meade, *An Introduction to Economic Analysis and Policy* (Oxford: Clarendon Press, 1936), 182–86; American edition by C. J. Hitch (New York: Oxford University Press, 1938), 195–99.

erable interest and has already found its way into some textbooks on public utility economics.[4] But despite the importance
of its practical implications, its paradoxical character, and the
fact that there are many economists who consider it fallacious,
it has so far received little written criticism.[5] It may have been
the sheer quantity of literature in favour of this solution and
the relatively small amount of written adverse criticism which
led J. M. Fleming to claim that it "is not, I think, open to
serious criticism" and to lament the fact that it was not more
widely understood and accepted "outside the narrow ranks of
the economists." But a different solution, which I believe in
essentials to be the correct one, had already been suggested
by C. L. Paine in 1937[6] and by E. W. Clemens in 1941.[7] I wrote

4. See C. Woody Thompson and Wendell R. Smith, *Public Utility Eco-
nomics* (New York: McGraw-Hill, 1941), 271–73, and Irston R. Barnes, *The
Economics of Public Utility Regulation* (New York: F. S. Crofts & Co., 1942),
586–88. See also Emery Troxel, "I: Incremental Cost Determination of Utility
Prices," "II: Limitations of the Incremental Cost Patterns of Pricing," "III:
Incremental Cost Control under Public Ownership," *Journal of Land and
Public Utility Economics* (November 1942, February 1943, and August 1943);
and James C. Bonbright, "Major Controversies as to the Criteria of Reasonable Public Utility Rates," *Papers and Proceedings,* American Economic Association (December 1940). Bonbright points out that the "extreme social
conservatism of most public utility and railroad specialists had prevented"
this solution "from gaining wide acceptance, or even from receiving any considerable notice, in the literature of rate theory." However, he thought that it
might become a live issue in the next few years (after 1940) as a result of
Hotelling's article, which Bonbright considered to be "one of the most distinguished contributions to rate-making theory in the entire literature of
economics."

5. It is true that Ragnar Frisch criticized Hotelling's article shortly after
it appeared. But, though much of interest emerged in Frisch's note and the
subsequent discussion with Hotelling, it appears, at least to the non-mathematical
reader, that Frisch's attack was not directed at the foundations of Hotelling's
argument but rather to what seemed to him to be defects in its formulation.
See Ragnar Frisch, "The Dupuit Taxation Theorem" (145–50) and "A Further
Note on the Dupuit Taxation Theorem" (156–57) and H. Hotelling, "The
Relation of Prices to Marginal Costs in an Optimum System" (151–55) and
"A Final Note" (158–60), all in *Econometrica* 7, no. 2 (April 1939).

6. See C. L. Paine, "Some Aspects of Discrimination by Public Utilities," *Economica,* n.s., 4, no. 16 (November 1937): 425–39.

7. See E. W. Clemens, "Price Discrimination in Decreasing Cost Industries," *American Economic Review* 31, no. 4 (December 1941): 794–802.

in 1945 a short note criticizing the solution as set out by Meade and Fleming,[8] and a further note by T. Wilson[9] underlined the fact that agreement among economists had not yet been reached. I now propose to examine the Hotelling-Lerner solution, as I shall call it, in greater detail and to point out the fundamental defects which I believe it contains.

II. Isolation of the Problem

Any actual economic situation is complex and a single economic problem does not exist in isolation. Consequently, confusion is liable to result because economists dealing with an actual situation are attempting to solve several problems at once. I believe this is true of the question I am discussing in this article. The central problem relates to a divergence between average and marginal costs. But in any actual case two other problems usually arise. First, some of the costs are common to numbers of consumers, and any consideration of the view that total costs ought to be borne by consumers raises the question of whether there is any rational method by which these common costs can be allocated among consumers. Secondly, many of the so-called fixed costs are in fact outlays which were made in the past for factors, the return to which in the present is a quasi-rent, and a consideration of what the return to such factors ought to be (in order to discover what total costs are) raises additional problems of great intricacy.[10] These are, I think, the other two problems which usually exist simultaneously with a divergence between average and marginal costs. They are, however, separate or at least separable questions. Thus, the example used by Hotelling, the problem of pricing in the case of a bridge,[11] is in fact an extremely

8. R. H. Coase, "Price and Output Policy of State Enterprise: A Comment," *Economic Journal* 55 (April 1945): 112–13.

9. T. Wilson, "Price and Output Policy of State Enterprise," *Economic Journal* 55 (December 1945): 454–61.

10. See F. A. Hayek, "The Present State of the Debate," in *Collectivist Economic Planning*, ed. F. A. Hayek (London: G. Routledge & Sons, 1935), 226–31.

11. This example was originally used by Dupuit in an article in the *Annales des Ponts et Chaussées* (1844) which was reprinted in *De l'utilité et de sa mesure* (Turin: La Riforma sociale, 1933).

complex case rather than the simple one it appears to be on the surface.

I propose to isolate the question at issue by examining an example in which, although there is a divergence between marginal and average costs, all costs are attributable to individual consumers; in which all costs are currently incurred; and in which, to avoid a further complication which might trouble some readers concerning the meaning of marginal cost, all factors are in perfectly elastic supply.

Assume that consumers are situated around a central market in which a certain product is available at constant prices. Assume that roads run out from the central market but that each road passes only one consumer of the product. Assume also that a carrier can carry on each journey additional units of the product at no additional cost (at least to a point beyond the limit of consumption of any individual consumer).[12] Assume further that the product is sold at the point of consumption. It is clear that the cost of supplying each individual consumer would be the cost of the carrier plus the cost at the central market of the number of units consumed by that particular consumer of the product. The marginal cost would be equal to the cost of a unit of the product at the central market. The average cost would be higher than the marginal cost and would decline as the cost of the carrier was spread over an increasing number of units.[13] The Hotelling-Lerner solution would presumably be that the amount which consumers should pay for each unit of the product should be equal only to marginal cost. The effect would be for consumers to pay for the cost of the product at the central market and for the govern-

12. An indivisibility must be present in all cases of decreasing average costs. Although I assume that it is not possible to employ less than a carrier, his services may be assumed to be in perfectly elastic supply in that payment will vary proportionately with the time he is employed and that the additional employment of carriers will not raise their price.

13. The assumption that the total costs consist of two distinct kinds, one of which enters into marginal cost while the other does not, is not essential. We could have assumed that the cost of carriage increased as additional units were carried but that the marginal costs of carriage were below the average. It will, however, aid in exposition if we keep to the original assumption.

ment, or rather the taxpayer, to bear the costs of carriage. It is the validity of this solution that I wish to examine. But first it is necessary to turn to a consideration of fundamentals.

III. What Is Optimum Pricing?

I take a pricing system to be one in which individual consumers have command over various sums of money which they use to obtain goods and services by spending this money in accordance with a system of prices. It is, of course, not the only method of allocating goods and services, or more properly, the use of factors of production between consumers. It would be possible for the government to decide what to produce and to allocate goods and services directly to consumers. But this would have disadvantages as compared with the use of a pricing system. No government could distinguish in any detail among the varying tastes of individual consumers (which is, of course, why a "points" system of rationing in wartime is adopted for many items);[14] without a pricing system, a most useful guide to what consumers' preferences really are would be lacking; furthermore, although a pricing system puts additional marketing costs on to consumers and firms, these may in fact be less than the organizing costs which would otherwise have to be incurred by the government.[15] These are the reasons which would lead an enlightened government to adopt a pricing system—and we shall see later that they are very relevant to the problem we are considering.

If it is decided to use a pricing system, there are two main problems that have to be solved. The first is, how much money shall each individual consumer have—the problem of the optimum distribution of income and wealth. The second is, what is to be the system of prices in accordance with which goods and services are to be made available to consumers—the problem of the optimum system of prices. It is with the second of these problems that I am concerned in this article. The first is partly, though not entirely, a question of ethics. But it is important to realize that there are these *two* problems and that

14. Cf. also Lerner, *Economics of Control,* 53.
15. See "The Nature of the Firm," 33–55.

both have to be solved if a pricing system is to produce satisfactory results. As I am in this section dealing with the second only of these problems, I shall assume that the distribution of income and wealth can be taken to be the optimum.

For an individual consumer, the system of prices represents the terms on which he can obtain various goods and services. According to what principles should prices be determined? The first would appear to be that for each individual consumer the same factor should have the same price in whatever use it is employed, since otherwise consumers would not be able to choose rationally, on the basis of price, the use in which they prefer a factor to be employed. The second would appear to be that the price of a factor should be the same for all consumers, since otherwise one consumer would be obtaining more for the same amount of money than another consumer. If the optimum distribution of income and wealth had been obtained, the effect of charging different prices for the same factor to different people would be to upset that distribution. It is a more subtle application of this second rule that the price fixed should be such as to allow factors to go to the highest bidders. That is, the price should be one which equates supply and demand and it should be the same for all consumers and in all uses.[16] This implies that the amount paid for a product should be equal to the value of the factors used in its production in another use or to another user. But the value of the factors used in the production of a product in another use or to another user is the cost of the product. We thus arrive at the familiar but important conclusion that the amount paid for a product should be equal to its cost. It will be this principle which will enable us to discuss the problems of individual pricing without tracing throughout the economic system all the changes consequent upon the alteration of a single price.

IV. The Argument for Multi-Part Pricing

How does this general argument for basing prices on costs apply to the case we are considering—the case of decreasing average costs? The writers whose views I am considering seem

16. Cf. also Lerner, *Economics of Control*, 45–50.

to assume that the alternatives with which one is faced are to charge a price equal to marginal cost (in which case a loss is made) or to charge a price equal to average cost (in which case no loss is made). There is, however, a third possibility—multi-part pricing. In this section I set out the argument for multi-part pricing when there are conditions of decreasing average costs.

It is clear that if the consumer is not allowed to obtain at the marginal cost additional units of products produced under conditions of decreasing average costs, he is not being allowed to choose in a rational manner between spending his money on consuming additional units of the product and spending his money in some other way, since the amount which he would be called upon to spend to obtain additional units of the product would not reflect the value of the factors in another use or to another user. But for the same reason it can be argued that the consumer should pay the total cost of the product. A consumer does not only have to decide whether to consume additional units of a product; he has also to decide whether it is worth his while to consume the product at all rather than spend his money in some other direction. This can be discovered if the consumer is asked to pay an amount equal to the total costs of supplying him, that is, an amount equal to the total value of the factors used in providing him with the product. If we apply this argument to our example, the consumer should not only pay the costs of obtaining additional units of the product at the central market; he should also pay the cost of carriage. How can this be brought about? The obvious answer is that the consumer should be charged one sum to cover the cost of carriage, while for additional units he should be charged the cost of the goods at the central market. We thus arrive at the conclusion that the form of pricing which is appropriate is a multi-part pricing system (in the particular case considered, a two-part pricing system), a type of pricing well known to students of public utilities and often advocated for just the reasons which I have set out in this article.[17]

17. See H. F. Havlik, *Service Charges in Gas and Electric Rates* (New York: Columbia University Press, 1938), and references therein. See also Barnes, *Public Utility Regulation,* 588. Havlik himself appears to support the view that

Now it is, I think, extremely significant that none of the advocates of the Hotelling-Lerner solution should have examined the possibilities of multi-part pricing as a solution of the problem they are considering. They write as though the only possible method of pricing is to charge a single price per unit and the problem they have to solve is what that price should be. It may be that their reason for not examining multi-part systems of pricing was that they were sure they had in fact found the optimum system of pricing. We must therefore compare the results of adopting the Hotelling-Lerner solution with those of using multi-part pricing.

V. Multi-Part Pricing Compared with the Hotelling-Lerner Solution

The Hotelling-Lerner solution, if adopted in the case of my example, would mean that the cost of the goods at the central market would be paid for by consumers but that the cost of carriage would be borne out of taxation. My objections to this solution as compared with adopting a two-part system of pricing fall under three heads: first, that it leads to a maldistribution of the factors of production among different uses; second, that it leads to a redistribution of income; and third, that the additional taxation imposed will tend to produce other harmful effects.

First, the Hotelling-Lerner solution would appear to remove the means whereby consumers make a rational choice

---

costs which are attributable to individual consumers should be charged to those consumers. He does, however, use a variant of the Hotelling-Lerner solution when dealing with the case in which what he terms marginal customer costs, "the additional costs of taking on a customer and maintaining the connection, without actually supplying him with electricity," are less than average customer costs. In this case, "revenues from a customer charge would be less than total customer costs" and it would be "justifiable" for the government "to give a subsidy" (pp. 92–93). Havlik does not discuss how the subsidy ought to be raised. In this article I am, however, concerned simply with the case in which all costs are attributable to individual consumers and to this case Havlik's variant of the Hotelling-Lerner solution, which is concerned with common costs, does not apply.

between the use as carriers and the use for some other purpose of the factors which enter into the cost of carriage. In this use, the factor would be free; in another use (provided that it entered into marginal cost) it would have to be paid for. Similarly, this solution would mean that consumers would choose between different locations without taking into account that the costs of carriage vary between one location and another.

The answer which the supporters of the Hotelling-Lerner solution would make to this objection would appear to be that the government should estimate for each individual consumer in my example whether he would buy the product and also what location he would prefer, if he had to pay the total cost.[18] Only if the consumer would thus have been prepared to pay the total cost of supplying the product to a given location will provision for supplying it to that location be made under the Hotelling-Lerner scheme. Hotelling points out that to decide whether the demand was sufficient to warrant the costs of building a bridge "would be a matter of estimation of vehicular and pedestrian traffic originating and terminating in particular zones, with a comparison of distances by alternative routes in each case, and an evaluation of the saving in each class of movement."[19] If it were possible to make such estimates, at low cost and with considerable accuracy and without knowledge of what had happened in the past when consumers had been required to pay the total cost, this would be likely to lead, in my opinion, not to a modification of the pricing system but rather to its abolition. The pricing system, as I pointed out earlier, is a particular method of allocating the use of factors of production among consumers, and the arguments for its adoption derive their main force from the view that such estimates of individual demand by a government would be very inaccurate. It should be noted here that neither Lerner nor Meade in fact make any considerable claim for the accuracy

18. See Lerner, *Economics of Control,* 186–99 and Meade, *Economic Analysis and Policy,* 324–25. And it would seem that Hotelling's mathematical formulation comes to much the same thing; see Hotelling, "General Welfare," 262, 268.

19. Hotelling, "General Welfare," 247–48.

of these estimates. Indeed, Lerner in an earlier section of his book argues for a pricing system on precisely the grounds that it is impossible for a government to make such estimates.[20]

Neither Hotelling nor Lerner nor Meade give, in my view, sufficient weight to the stimulus to correct forecasting, which comes from having a subsequent market test of whether consumers are willing to pay the total cost of the product. Nor do they recognize the importance of the aid which the results of this market test give in enabling more accurate forecasts to be made in the future. Hotelling says: "Defenders of the current theory that the overhead costs of an industry must be met out of the sale of its products or services hold that this is necessary in order to find out whether the creation of the industry was a wise social policy. Nothing could be more absurd." This, he says, "is an interesting historical question."[21] And he adds later: "When the question arises of building new railroads or new major industries of any kind or of scrapping the old, we shall face, not a historical, but a mathematical and economic problem."[22] Nowhere in Hotelling's article does one find recognition of the fact that it will be more difficult to discover whether to build new railroads or new industries if one does not know whether the creation of past railroads or industries was wise social policy. And it is certainly not absurd to take into account the fact that decisions are likely to be better made if afterwards there is some test of whether such decisions were wise social policy than if such an enquiry is never made.

I do not myself believe that a government could make accurate estimates of individual demand in a regime in which all prices were based on marginal costs. But it may be well to consider what would be likely to be done if a government attempted to carry out the Hotelling-Lerner policy. Consider the example I have been discussing. Certain consumers would have to be designated as able to buy the product. The government would then undertake to pay whatever costs for carriage were incurred on behalf of these consumers. A government

20. Lerner, *Economics of Control*, 61–64.
21. Hotelling, "General Welfare," 268.
22. Ibid., 269.

would have a difficult task in deciding where to draw the line. If it adopted a narrow view of the qualifications required of those allowed to consume this product, consumers who really preferred to use the factor employed in the carriage of the product in this way would be prevented from doing so. If on the other hand it was liberal in its view, many would find that they were no longer deterred from consuming the product or living at a greater distance from the central market by the cost of the factor used in carriage, that is, by its value in alternative uses or to an alternative user. It would, of course, be possible for the government to follow a liberal policy to one class of consumers and a narrow policy to others at the same time. It is not easy to guess what policy a government would be likely to follow. But in Great Britain I suspect that it would tend to err on the liberal side and that there would consequently be too great an employment of the factor used in the carriage of the product.[23]

But even if the government were able to estimate individual demands accurately, the Hotelling-Lerner solution would be subject to another objection. The government is supposed to estimate which consumers would be willing to pay the cost of carriage (and we shall assume for the moment that it estimates correctly). But it does not in fact ask these consumers to pay this sum. This money is then available for these consumers to spend on some other commodity. Consumers who buy products which are produced under conditions of decreasing average costs will therefore obtain products for any given expenditure embodying a greater value of factors than those who do not. There is a redistribution of income in favour of consumers of goods produced under conditions of decreasing average costs.[24]

23. All the essentials of this argument have been set out in another connection by Edwin Cannan in his *The History of Local Rates in England*, 2nd ed. (London: P. S. King & Son, 1912). See chapter 8, "The Economy of Local Rates," and especially his remarks on p. 187.

24. This assumes that the taxes from which the loss is made good do not fall entirely on consumers of goods produced under conditions of decreasing average costs. This is, of course, so because it is proposed that the taxes to be used should be income and similar taxes.

There would not, I think, be any dispute that what is equivalent to a redistribution of income does in these circumstances take place. Hotelling is, however, the only one of the writers whose views I am examining who deals explicitly with this point. I shall therefore examine his reasons for thinking that this objection is of little substance. First of all, I believe that Hotelling considers this objection to be largely irrelevant because the initial distribution of income, at least in the United States, is not in fact the optimum. He does not directly say this but it is evident from his whole approach to the question.[25] When he argues that the loss resulting from an application of the marginal cost rule should be borne out of income taxes, inheritance taxes, and taxes on the site value of land, he is, I think, doing so partly because he believes that the wealthy and the landlords already have too large a share of the total wealth and income. But why should consumers of goods produced under conditions of decreasing average costs be the only ones to benefit from this redistribution? The reason why Hotelling sees little harm in using pricing policy partly as a means of redistributing income is, I think, that he does not consider the distinction between consumers of products produced under conditions of decreasing average costs and consumers of products produced under conditions of constant or increasing average costs to be of great importance. He argues that a government carrying out his policy would undertake a great variety of public works. "A rough randomness in distribution would be ample to ensure such a distribution of benefits that most persons in every part of the country would be better off by reason of the programme as a whole."[26] This comes to saying that, in a regime of marginal cost pricing, all consumers will buy goods produced under conditions of decreasing average costs; that what is lost by any particular consumer in the redistribution involved in one scheme will be offset as a result of the redistribution following on another scheme; and that, as a consequence, the significant redistribution would be from the wealthy and landlords to all others. It would be indeed pedantic

25. See, for example, his remarks in "General Welfare," 259.
26. Ibid.

to object to the achievement of a desirable aim merely because it is done in an unusual way. But this argument stands or falls by the assumption that there will be no significant redistribution among consumers of different kinds of products. There is no reason to assume that this will be so. The gain which individual consumers would derive from the Hotelling-Lerner policy would depend on the extent to which they were willing to pay the total cost for products produced under conditions of decreasing average costs (given their initial income); and on the absolute divergence between marginal and average costs in the case of these goods; and on the extent to which the additional income derived as a result of the Hotelling-Lerner policy was spent on goods produced under conditions of decreasing average costs; and on the absolute divergence between marginal and average costs in these cases. It would be possible to appraise the character of the redistribution only after a detailed factual enquiry. There seems, however, to be no reason to suppose that it would be a negligible redistribution.

The public utility industries provide some of the most striking instances of products supplied under conditions of decreasing average costs. Let us assume that they are the only industries in which these conditions are found. Consumers who live in regions of low density of population would probably not be willing to pay the total costs of supply of public utility services, which in their case would be very high, and they would consequently gain nothing as a result of the Hotelling-Lerner policy because they would not be given the services. Consumers who live in cities would find their gains limited because, equipment there being relatively intensively used, the divergence between marginal and average cost would probably be much less than elsewhere; while since they probably already use all the public utility services, the additional income would be likely to be spent on other than public utility services. It would be those living in small towns that have some but not all the public utility services, where the divergence between marginal and average cost was great, who would, I think, tend to gain most from the Hotelling-Lerner policy. I see no reason to suppose that there would not be some redistribution, possibly very considerable, as a result of this policy if it were generally applied. Hotelling admits this possibility but claims that by a subsequent redistribution a situation could be produced in which everyone was better off than before.[27] He does not describe how this redistribution would be effected. But it would obviously be an inferior arrangement to adopting a multi-part system of pricing which makes it unnecessary to have subsequent redistributions of income at all. I am, however, at a loss to understand how ordinary taxation procedures could be used to redistribute income from consumers of goods produced under conditions of decreasing average costs to all other consumers. An attempt to do this might be made by means of a tax on the consumption of goods produced under conditions of decreasing average costs. But either this would be equivalent to introducing multi-part pricing (if a lump sum tax was levied on consumers) or, if a tax per unit of consumption is imposed, it would bring about a divergence between the amount paid for additional units and marginal cost, a result which it is the object of the Hotelling-Lerner solution to avoid.

I now turn to the third objection to the Hotelling-Lerner solution. The loss incurred is, it is said, to be made good by increased taxation. The taxes which Hotelling and the others who support this solution have in mind are income taxes, inheritance taxes, and taxes on the site value of land. Let us assume for the time being that the form of tax used to make good the loss is an income tax. But income taxes are usually so framed that marginal units of income are taxed, and therefore an income tax will have the same unfortunate effect on consumers' choice as a tax on goods and will produce results similar in character to those which follow from charging an amount for additional units of output greater than marginal cost. After the appearance of Hotelling's first article, he seems to have had his attention drawn to this point by Lerner. Hotelling says in the discussion with Frisch which followed his original article that "an income tax of the usual kind is a sort of excise tax on effort and on waiting, as well as on other less defensible ways of getting an income. An income tax is to some extent objectionable because it affects the choice between ef-

27. Ibid., 257–58.

fort and leisure, and the choice between immediate and post-
poned consumption. Thus some of the same kind of loss at-
taches to an income tax as to excise taxes proper. How serious
this effect may be is a question for factual research; but there
is some reason to suppose an income tax superior to excise
taxes on individual commodities in this respect. . . ."[28] Hotelling does not give any reasons why he thinks income taxes
will tend to be less harmful in this respect than excise taxes.
It may be so, but it is obviously desirable to know what the
circumstances are in which income taxes are less harmful and
when they are likely to be found before applying the Hotelling-
Lerner solution—if, that is, this policy would lead to increases
in income taxes.[29] Hotelling attempts to avoid this difficulty
by suggesting that "the public revenues, including those required to operate industries with sales at marginal cost, should
. . . be derived primarily from rents of land and other scarce
goods, inheritance and windfall taxes, and taxes designed to
reduce socially harmful consumption."[30] This is not a very
satisfactory solution. First of all, it assumes that such taxes
will be sufficient to raise the sum required. Second, it assumes
that the disturbance to the distribution of income and wealth
due to the additional taxation on those who derive their incomes in these ways is better than the loss which would occur
if the additional taxation was spread more evenly over people
in the country. Alternatively, Hotelling's suggestion involves
the assumption that the optimum distribution of income and
wealth has not already been achieved and that those who derive

28. Hotelling, "Relation of Prices," 154–55. I would add that income
taxes also affect the choice between doing a job for oneself and employing
some one to do it for one and in consequence an income tax dissipates some
of the advantages of specialization. See F. W. Paish, "Economic Incentive in
Wartime," *Economica*, n.s., 8, no. 31 (August 1941): 244.

29. This problem seems to have been overlooked in the theory of public
finance. The usual discussion of the burden of indirect taxation assumes that
the alternative is a lump sum payment. See for example, M. F. W. Joseph,
"The Excess Burden of Indirect Taxation," *Review of Economic Studies* 6
(June 1939): 226–31. Cf. also J. R. Hicks, *Value and Capital* (Oxford: Clarendon Press, 1939), 41.

30. Hotelling, "Relation of Prices," 155.

their incomes in these ways have not been taxed enough in the past. But, of course, if this is so, this further taxation is desirable quite apart from questions of pricing policy, and there is little need to link it to the problem of pricing under conditions of decreasing average costs. Furthermore, the question would still remain of how the pricing problem should be solved when the optimum distribution of income and wealth was achieved. Hotelling's suggestion for avoiding the loss which would result from increased income taxes is one of limited validity.

In this section, I have compared the results of using a multi-part pricing system with those which would follow from the Hotelling-Lerner policy. I have shown that the Hotelling-Lerner solution would bring about a maldistribution of the factors of production, a maldistribution of income, and probably a loss similar to that which the scheme was designed to avoid, but arising out of the effect of increased income taxes. These results would be avoided by the use of a multi-part system of pricing.

VI. Average Cost Pricing Compared with the Hotelling-Lerner Solution

Hotelling, Lerner, Meade, and Fleming do not seem to have realized that many of the problems which they were trying to solve could have been dealt with by means of multi-part pricing, and that this system of pricing would in fact have produced results not open to the objections which could be brought against the Hotelling-Lerner solution. But in fairness to them, it must be pointed out that their attack was directed against charging a single price which was based on average cost and not against multi-part pricing. Is the argument valid in this case? If multi-part pricing is not possible, is it not preferable to adopt the Hotelling-Lerner solution rather than to adopt pricing based on average cost?

In this case, the argument for the Hotelling-Lerner solution is considerably strengthened—and this in two respects. First of all, it is clear that if consumers are not allowed to buy additional units at marginal cost, there is a maldistribution of the factors of production. The nature of the gain which would accrue in this respect through the adoption of the Hotelling-Lerner solution has already been discussed in earlier sections.[31] The second respect in which the argument for the Hotelling-Lerner solution is strengthened concerns the effectiveness of average cost pricing in providing a market test of the willingness of consumers to pay the total costs. In the previous section, I pointed out that multi-part pricing furnished such a test. How does this apply to the case of average cost pricing? The fact that consumers are willing to buy at a price which covers average costs certainly shows that they prefer to obtain that value of factors in that form rather than in any other which is open to them.[32] The difficulty is, as Hotelling points out, that the reverse is not true. It has long been known to economists that in cases in which the demand curve lies at all points below the average cost curve, it may be possible, by means of price discrimination, to raise the average revenue sufficiently to bring it up to average cost. If therefore pricing is on an average cost basis, there will be certain cases in which consumers would have been willing to pay the total cost but in which, owing to the limitations of this particular method of pricing, this would not be possible. Production could be undertaken in such cases if the Hotelling-Lerner policy was followed.

These are the advantages of the Hotelling-Lerner solution as compared with average cost pricing. But the disadvantages which were examined in the previous section still remain. These have to be balanced one against the other. The first advantage which the Hotelling-Lerner solution possesses as compared with average cost pricing is that it allows a better choice at the margin in consumption. But this advantage would be reduced

31. It might be thought that if all goods were priced on an average cost basis, since all prices would be raised above the marginal cost level, the choice of the consumers would be unaffected. But this would be true only if the rise in price were proportionate to marginal cost and this is most unlikely to be true. See the discussion between Frisch and Hotelling in *Econometrica* (April 1939).

32. Cf. Philip H. Wicksteed, *The Common Sense of Political Economy and Selected Papers and Reviews on Economic Theory,* vol. 2 (London: G. Routledge & Sons, 1933), 675–76.

and might be offset by the loss which would result if the Hotelling-Lerner solution involved increased income taxes. The second advantage is that a government could undertake production in cases in which consumers would be willing to pay the total cost but which could not be undertaken with average cost pricing. But it has to be remembered that this policy is one in which the government estimates individual demands and is therefore subject to the limitations which we discussed in the previous section. Not all cases in which production would not be undertaken with average cost pricing ought to be undertaken. A government which made many errors in its estimates of individual demands could easily offset any good such a policy might produce. Average cost pricing may prevent some things from being done which perhaps ought to be done, but it is also a means of avoiding certain errors in production, some of which would inevitably be made if the Hotelling-Lerner policy were followed. As I indicated earlier, I do not myself believe that it is reasonable to assume that the government could make accurate estimates of individual demands if all prices were based on marginal cost. Finally, there is the redistribution of income and wealth which the Hotelling-Lerner solution would involve and which, as I pointed out in the previous section, would appear to be difficult to rectify in the absence of multi-part pricing without reintroducing the kind of tax which would prevent that rational choice at the margin which the Hotelling-Lerner solution aims to achieve.

It will be seen from the discussion in this section that the question of average cost pricing against the Hotelling-Lerner solution does not present any clear-cut case. The claim which is made for the Hotelling-Lerner solution as inevitably superior to average cost pricing must therefore be rejected.

VII. The Problems that Remain

In this article, I have been examining the problem of pricing under conditions of decreasing average costs. I have, however, confined myself to one particular case, that in which all costs are attributable to individual consumers and in which all costs are currently incurred. Given these assumptions, I showed that the Hotelling-Lerner solution was inferior to a multi-part system of pricing and that, as compared with average cost pricing, the balance of advantage was not clear. The next steps would appear to be to examine the problem of pricing when there are common costs. If there are costs which cannot be attributed to individual consumers, does the Hotelling-Lerner solution then come into its own, as H. F. Havlik has suggested?[33] Should such common costs be borne out of taxation? Or is the right approach to discover some basis in accordance with which these costs should be allocated among consumers? Finally, there is the question of expenditures which have already been incurred for factors. Are these costs to be borne out of taxation? Or should they be borne by consumers? If the analysis in this article is accepted, these would seem to be the next questions to be examined.

33. See note 17.

FIVE

The Problem of Social Cost

I. The Problem to be Examined[1]

This paper is concerned with those actions of business firms which have harmful effects on others. The standard example is that of a factory, the smoke from which has harmful effects on those occupying neighbouring properties. The economic analysis of such a situation has usually proceeded in terms of a divergence between the private and social product of the factory, in which economists have largely followed the treatment of Pigou in *The Economics of Welfare*. The conclusions to which this kind of analysis seems to have led most economists is that it would be desirable to make the owner of the factory liable for the damage caused to those injured by the smoke; or to place a tax on the factory owner varying with the amount of smoke produced and equivalent in money terms to the damage it would cause; or, finally, to exclude the factory from residential districts (and presumably from other areas in which the emission of smoke would have harmful effects on

Reprinted from *The Journal of Law and Economics* 3 (October 1960): 1–44. ©1960 by The University of Chicago Press. All rights reserved.

1. This article, although concerned with a technical problem of economic analysis, arose out of the study of the Political Economy of Broadcasting. The argument of the present article was implicit in a previous article dealing with the problem of allocating radio and television frequencies ("The Federal Communications Commission," *The Journal of Law and Economics* 2 [October 1959], but comments which I have received seemed to suggest that it would be desirable to deal with the question in a more explicit way and without reference to the original problem for the solution of which the analysis was developed.

others). It is my contention that the suggested courses of action are inappropriate in that they lead to results which are not necessarily, or even usually, desirable.

II. The Reciprocal Nature of the Problem

The traditional approach has tended to obscure the nature of the choice that has to be made. The question is commonly thought of as one in which A inflicts harm on B and what has to be decided is, How should we restrain A? But this is wrong. We are dealing with a problem of a reciprocal nature. To avoid the harm to B would be to inflict harm on A. The real question that has to be decided is, Should A be allowed to harm B or should B be allowed to harm A? The problem is to avoid the more serious harm. I instanced in my previous article[2] the case of a confectioner, the noise and vibrations from whose machinery disturbed a doctor in his work. To avoid harming the doctor would be to inflict harm on the confectioner. The problem posed by this case was essentially whether it was worth while, as a result of restricting the methods of production which could be used by the confectioner, to secure more doctoring at the cost of a reduced supply of confectionery products. Another example is afforded by the problem of straying cattle which destroy crops on neighbouring land. If it is inevitable that some cattle will stray, an increase in the supply of meat can only be obtained at the expense of a decrease in the supply of crops. The nature of the choice is clear: meat or crops. What answer should be given is, of course, not clear unless we know the value of what is obtained as well as the value of what is sacrificed to obtain it. To give another example, George J. Stigler instances the contamination of a stream.[3] If we assume that the harmful effect of the pollution is that it kills the fish, the question to be decided is, Is the value of the fish lost greater or less than the value of the product which the contamination of the stream makes possible? It goes almost without saying that this problem has to be looked at in total and at the margin.

2. Coase, "Federal Communications Commission," 26–27.
3. George J. Stigler, *The Theory of Price*, rev. ed. (New York: Macmillan Co., 1952), 105.

III. The Pricing System with Liability for Damage

I propose to start my analysis by examining a case in which most economists would presumably agree that the problem would be solved in a completely satisfactory manner: when the damaging business has to pay for all damage caused and the pricing system works smoothly (strictly this means that the operation of a pricing system is without cost).

A good example of the problem under discussion is afforded by the case of straying cattle which destroy crops growing on neighbouring land. Let us suppose that a farmer and a cattle-raiser are operating on neighbouring properties. Let us further suppose that, without any fencing between the properties, an increase in the size of the cattle-raiser's herd increases the total damage to the farmer's crops. What happens to the marginal damage as the size of the herd increases is another matter. This depends on whether the cattle tend to follow one another or to roam side by side, on whether they tend to be more or less restless as the size of the herd increases, and on other similar factors. For my immediate purpose, it is immaterial what assumption is made about marginal damage as the size of the herd increases.

To simplify the argument, I propose to use an arithmetical example. I shall assume that the annual cost of fencing the farmer's property is $9 and that the price of the crop is $1 per ton. Also, I assume that the relation between the number of cattle in the herd and the annual crop loss is as follows:

Number in Herd (Steers)	Annual Crop Loss (Tons)	Crop Loss per Additional Steer (Tons)
1	1	1
2	3	2
3	6	3
4	10	4

Given that the cattle-raiser is liable for the damage caused, the additional annual cost imposed on the cattle-raiser if he increased his herd from, say, 2 to 3 steers is $3, and in deciding on the size of the herd, he will take this into account along with his other costs. That is, he will not increase the size of the herd unless the value of the additional meat produced (assuming that the cattle-raiser slaughters the cattle) is greater than the additional costs that this will entail, including the value of the additional crops destroyed. Of course, if, by the employment of dogs, herdsmen, aeroplanes, mobile radio, and other means, the amount of damage can be reduced, these means will be adopted when their cost is less than the value of the crop which they prevent being lost. Given that the annual cost of fencing is $9, the cattle-raiser who wished to have a herd with 4 steers or more would pay for fencing to be erected and maintained, assuming that other means of attaining the same end would not do so more cheaply. When the fence is erected, the marginal cost due to the liability for damage becomes zero, except to the extent that an increase in the size of the herd necessitates a stronger and therefore more expensive fence because more steers are liable to lean against it at the same time. But, of course, it may be cheaper for the cattle-raiser not to fence and to pay for the damaged crops, as in my arithmetical example, with 3 or fewer steers.

It might be thought that the fact that the cattle-raiser would pay for all crops damaged would lead the farmer to increase his planting if a cattle-raiser came to occupy the neighbouring property. But this is not so. If the crop was previously sold in conditions of perfect competition, marginal cost was equal to price for the amount of planting undertaken, and any expansion would have reduced the profits of the farmer. In the new situation, the existence of crop damage would mean that the farmer would sell less on the open market, but his receipts for a given production would remain the same since the cattle-raiser would pay the market price for any crop damaged. Of course, if cattle-raising commonly involved the destruction of crops, the coming into existence of a cattle-raising industry might raise the price of the crops involved and farmers would then extend their planting. But I wish to confine my attention to the individual farmer.

I have said that the occupation of a neighbouring property by a cattle-raiser would not cause the amount of production, or perhaps more exactly the amount of planting, by the farmer to increase. In fact, if the cattle-raising has any effect, it will be to decrease the amount of planting. The reason for this is that, for any given tract of land, if the value of the crop damaged is so great that the receipts from the sale of the undamaged crop are less than the total costs of cultivating that tract of land, it will be profitable for the farmer and the cattle-raiser to make a bargain whereby that tract of land is left uncultivated. This can be made clear by means of an arithmetical example. Assume initially that the value of the crop obtained from cultivating a given tract of land is \$12 and that the cost incurred in cultivating this tract of land is \$10, the net gain from cultivating the land being \$2. I assume for purposes of simplicity that the farmer owns the land. Now assume that the cattle-raiser starts operations on the neighbouring property and that the value of the crops damaged is \$1. In this case \$11 is obtained by the farmer from sale on the market and \$1 is obtained from the cattle-raiser for damage suffered and the net gain remains \$2. Now suppose that the cattle-raiser finds it profitable to increase the size of his herd, even though the amount of damage rises to \$3; which means that the value of the additional meat production is greater than the additional costs, including the additional \$2 payment for damage. But the total payment for damage is now \$3. The net gain to the farmer from cultivating the land is still \$2. The cattle-raiser would be better off if the farmer would agree not to cultivate his land for any payment less than \$3. The farmer would be agreeable to not cultivating the land for any payment greater than \$2. There is clearly room for a mutually satisfactory bargain which would lead to the abandonment of cultivation.[4] But the same argument applies

4. The argument in the text has proceeded on the assumption that the alternative to cultivation of the crop is abandonment of cultivation altogether. But this need not be so. There may be crops which are less liable to damage by cattle but which would not be as profitable as the crop grown in the absence of damage. Thus, if the cultivation of a new crop would yield a return to the farmer of \$1 instead of \$2, and the size of the herd which would cause \$3 damage with the old crop would cause \$1 damage with the new crop, it would be profitable to the cattle-raiser to pay any sum less than \$2 to induce the farmer to change his crop (since this would reduce damage liability from \$3 to \$1) and it would be profitable for the farmer to do so if the amount received was more than \$1 (the reduction in his return caused by switching crops). In

not only to the whole tract cultivated by the farmer but also to any subdivision of it. Suppose, for example, that the cattle have a well-defined route, say, to a brook or to a shady area. In these circumstances, the amount of damage to the crop along the route may well be great; and if so, it could be that the farmer and the cattle-raiser would find it profitable to make a bargain whereby the farmer would agree not to cultivate this strip of land.

But this raises a further possibility. Suppose that there is such a well-defined route. Suppose further that the value of the crop that would be obtained by cultivating this strip of land is $10 but that the cost of cultivation is $11. In the absence of the cattle-raiser, the land would not be cultivated. However, given the presence of the cattle-raiser, it could well be that if the strip was cultivated, the whole crop would be destroyed by the cattle. In this case, the cattle-raiser would be forced to pay $10 to the farmer. It is true that the farmer would lose $1. But the cattle-raiser would lose $10. Clearly this is a situation which is not likely to last indefinitely since neither party would want this to happen. The aim of the farmer would be to induce the cattle-raiser to make a payment in return for an agreement to leave this land uncultivated. The farmer would not be able to obtain a payment greater than the cost of fencing off this piece of land nor so high as to lead the cattle-raiser to abandon the use of the neighbouring property. What payment would in fact be made would depend on the shrewdness of the farmer and the cattle-raiser as bargainers. But as the payment would not be so high as to cause the cattle-raiser to abandon this location and as it would not vary with the size of the herd, such an agreement would not affect the allocation of resources but would merely alter the distribution of income and wealth between the cattle-raiser and the farmer.

I think it is clear that if the cattle-raiser is liable for damage caused and the pricing system works smoothly, the reduction

---

fact, there would be room for a mutually satisfactory bargain in all cases in which a change of crop would reduce the amount of damage by more than it reduces the value of the crop (excluding damage)—in all cases, that is, in which a change in the crop cultivated would lead to an increase in the value of production.

in the value of production elsewhere will be taken into account in computing the additional cost involved in increasing the size of the herd This cost will be weighed against the value of the additional meat production and, given perfect competition in the cattle industry, the allocation of resources in cattle-raising will be optimal. What needs to be emphasized is that the fall in the value of production elsewhere which would be taken into account in the costs of the cattle-raiser may well be less than the damage which the cattle would cause to the crops in the ordinary course of events. This is because it is possible, as a result of market transactions, to discontinue cultivation of the land. This is desirable in all cases in which the damage that the cattle would cause, and for which the cattle-raiser would be willing to pay, exceeds the amount which the farmer would pay for use of the land. In conditions of perfect competition, the amount which the farmer would pay for the use of the land is equal to the difference between the value of the total production when factors are employed on this land and the value of the additional product yielded in their next best use (which would be what the farmer would have to pay for the factors). If damage exceeds the amount the farmer would pay for the use of the land, the value of the additional product of the factors employed elsewhere would exceed the value of the total product in this use after damage is taken into account. It follows that it would be desirable to abandon cultivation of the land and to release the factors employed for production elsewhere. A procedure which merely provided for payment for damage to the crop caused by the cattle but which did not allow for the possibility of cultivation being discontinued would result in too small an employment of factors of production in cattle-raising and too large an employment of factors in cultivation of the crop. But with the possibility of market transactions, a situation in which damage to crops exceeded the rent of the land would not endure. Whether the cattle-raiser pays the farmer to have the land uncultivated or himself rents the land by paying the land-owner an amount slightly greater than the farmer would pay (if the farmer was himself renting the land), the final result would be the same and would maximize the value of production. Even when the farmer is induced to plant crops which would not be profitable to cultivate for sale on the market, this will be a purely short-term phenomenon and may be expected to lead to an agreement under which the planting will cease. The cattle-raiser will remain in that location and the marginal cost of meat production will be the same as before, thus having no long-run effect on the allocation of resources.

IV. The Pricing System with no Liability for Damage

I now turn to the case in which, although the pricing system is assumed to work smoothly (that is, costlessly), the damaging business is not liable for any of the damage which it causes. This business does not have to make a payment to those damaged by its actions. I propose to show that the allocation of resources will be the same in this case as it was when the damaging business was liable for damage caused. As I showed in the previous case that the allocation of resources was optimal, it will not be necessary to repeat this part of the argument.

I return to the case of the farmer and the cattle-raiser. The farmer would suffer increased damage to his crop as the size of the herd increased. Suppose that the size of the cattle-raiser's herd is three steers (and that this is the size of the herd that would be maintained if crop damage was not taken into account). Then the farmer would be willing to pay up to $3 if the cattle-raiser would reduce his herd to two steers, up to $5 if the herd were reduced to one steer, and up to $6 if cattle-raising was abandoned. The cattle-raiser would therefore receive $3 from the farmer if he kept two steers instead of three. This $3 foregone is therefore part of the cost incurred in keeping the third steer. Whether the $3 is a payment which the cattle-raiser has to make if he adds the third steer to his herd (which it would be if the cattle-raiser was liable to the farmer for damage caused to the crop) or whether it is a sum of money which he would have received if he did not keep a third steer (which it would be if the cattle-raiser was not liable to the farmer for damage caused to the crop) does not affect the final result. In both cases $3 is part of the cost of adding a third steer, to be included along with the other costs. If the increase in the value of production in cattle-raising through increasing the size of the herd from two to three is greater than the additional costs that have to be incurred (including the $3 damage to crops), the size of the herd will be increased. Otherwise, it will not. The size of the herd will be the same whether the cattle-raiser is liable for damage caused to the crop or not.

It may be argued that the assumed starting point—a herd of three steers—was arbitrary. And this is true. But the farmer would not wish to pay to avoid crop damage which the cattle-raiser would not be able to cause. For example, the maximum annual payment which the farmer could be induced to pay could not exceed $9, the annual cost of fencing. And the farmer would only be willing to pay this sum if it did not reduce his earnings to a level that would cause him to abandon cultivation of this particular tract of land. Furthermore, the farmer would only be willing to pay this amount if he believed that, in the absence of any payment by him, the size of the herd maintained by the cattle-raiser would be four or more steers. Let us assume that this is the case. Then the farmer would be willing to pay up to $3 if the cattle-raiser would reduce his herd to three steers, up to $6 if the herd were reduced to two steers, up to $8 if one steer only were kept, and up to $9 if cattle-raising were abandoned. It will be noticed that the change in the starting point has not altered the amount which would accrue to the cattle-raiser if he reduced the size of his herd by any given amount. It is still true that the cattle-raiser could receive an additional $3 from the farmer if he agreed to reduce his herd from three steers to two and that the $3 represents the value of the crop that would be destroyed by adding the third steer to the herd. Although a different belief on the part of the farmer (whether justified or not) about the size of the herd that the cattle-raiser would maintain in the absence of payments from him may affect the total payment he can be induced to pay, it is not true that this different belief would have any effect on the size of the herd that the cattle-raiser will actually keep. This will be the same as it would be if the cattle-raiser had to pay for damage caused by his cattle, since a receipt foregone of a given amount is the equivalent of a payment of the same amount.

It might be thought that it would pay the cattle-raiser to increase his herd above the size that he would wish to maintain once a bargain had been made, in order to induce the farmer to make a larger total payment. And this may be true. It is similar in nature to the action of the farmer (when the cattle-raiser was liable for damage) in cultivating land on which, as a result of an agreement with the cattle-raiser, planting would subsequently be abandoned (including land which would not be cultivated at all in the absence of cattle-raising). But such manoeuvres are preliminaries to an agreement and do not affect the long-run equilibrium position, which is the same whether or not the cattle-raiser is held responsible for the crop damage brought about by his cattle.

It is necessary to know whether the damaging business is liable or not for damage caused, since without the establishment of this initial delimitation of rights there can be no market transactions to transfer and recombine them. But the ultimate result (which maximizes the value of production) is independent of the legal position if the pricing system is assumed to work without cost.

V. The Problem Illustrated Anew

The harmful effects of the activities of a business can assume a wide variety of forms. An early English case concerned a building which, by obstructing currents of air, hindered the operation of a windmill.[5] A recent case in Florida concerned a building which cast a shadow on the cabana, swimming pool, and sunbathing areas of a neighbouring hotel.[6] The problem of straying cattle and the damaging of crops which was the subject of detailed examination in the two preceding sections, although it may have appeared to be rather a special case, is in fact but one example of a problem which arises in many different guises. To clarify the nature of my argument and to demonstrate its

5. See *Gale on Easements,* 13th ed. M. Bowles (London: Sweet & Maxwell, 1959) 237–39.

6. See Fountainbleu Hotel Corp. v. Forty-Five Twenty-Five, Inc., 114 So. 2d 357 (1959).

general applicability, I propose to illustrate it anew by reference to four actual cases.

Let us first reconsider the case of *Sturges v. Bridgman*,[7] which I used as an illustration of the general problem in my article on "The Federal Communications Commission." In this case, a confectioner (in Wigmore Street) used two mortars and pestles in connection with his business (one had been in operation in the same position for more than sixty years and the other for more than twenty-six years). A doctor then came to occupy neighbouring premises (in Wimpole Street). The confectioner's machinery caused the doctor no harm until, eight years after he had first occupied the premises, he built a consulting room at the end of his garden right against the confectioner's kitchen. It was then found that the noise and vibration caused by the confectioner's machinery made it difficult for the doctor to use his new consulting room. "In particular . . . the noise prevented him from examining his patients by auscultation[8] for diseases of the chest. He also found it impossible to engage with effect in any occupation which required thought and attention." The doctor therefore brought a legal action to force the confectioner to stop using his machinery. The courts had little difficulty in granting the doctor the injunction he sought. "Individual cases of hardship may occur in the strict carrying out of the principle upon which we found our judgment, but the negation of the principle would lead even more to individual hardship, and would at the same time produce a prejudicial effect upon the development of land for residential purposes."

The court's decision established that the doctor had the right to prevent the confectioner from using his machinery. But, of course, it would have been possible to modify the arrangements envisaged in the legal ruling by means of a bargain between the parties. The doctor would have been willing to waive his right and allow the machinery to continue in operation if the confectioner would have paid him a sum of money

---

7. Sturges v. Bridgman, 1 Ch. D. 852 (1879).

8. Auscultation is the act of listening by ear or stethoscope in order to judge by sound the condition of the body.

which was greater than the loss of income which he would suffer from having to move to a more costly or less convenient location, from having to curtail his activities at this location, or (and this was suggested as a possibility) from having to build a separate wall which would deaden the noise and vibration. The confectioner would have been willing to do this if the amount he would have had to pay the doctor was less than the fall in income he would suffer if he had to change his mode of operation at this location, abandon his operation, or move his confectionery business to some other location. The solution of the problem depends essentially on whether the continued use of the machinery adds more to the confectioner's income than it subtracts from the doctor's.[9] But now consider the situation if the confectioner had won the case. The confectioner would then have had the right to continue operating his noise- and vibration-generating machinery without having to pay anything to the doctor. The boot would have been on the other foot: the doctor would have had to pay the confectioner to induce him to stop using the machinery. If the doctor's income would have fallen more through continuance of the use of this machinery than it added to the income of the confectioner, there would clearly be room for a bargain whereby the doctor paid the confectioner to stop using the machinery. That is to say, the circumstances in which it would not pay the confectioner to continue to use the machinery and to compensate the doctor for the losses that this would bring (if the doctor had the right to prevent the confectioner's using his machinery) would be those in which it would be in the interest of the doctor to make a payment to the confectioner which would induce him to discontinue the use of the machinery (if the confectioner had the right to operate the machinery). The basic conditions are exactly the same in this case as they were in the example of the cattle which destroyed crops. With costless market transactions, the decision of the courts concerning liability for damage would be without effect on the allocation of resources. It was

9. Note that what is taken into account is the change in income after allowing for alterations in methods of production, location, character of product, etc.

of course the view of the judges that they were affecting the working of the economic system—and in a desirable direction. Any other decision would have had "a prejudicial effect upon the development of land for residential purposes," an argument which was elaborated by examining the example of a forge operating on a barren moor which was later developed for residential purposes. The judges' view that they were settling how the land was to be used would be true only in the case in which the costs of carrying out the necessary market transactions exceeded the gain which might be achieved by any arrangement of rights. And it would be desirable to preserve the areas (Wimpole Street or the moor) for residential or professional use (by giving non-industrial users the right to stop the noise, vibration, smoke, etc., by injunction) only if the value of the additional residential facilities obtained was greater than the value of cakes or iron lost. But of this the judges seem to have been unaware.

Another example of the same problem is furnished by the case of *Cooke v. Forbes*.[10] One process in the weaving of cocoanut fibre matting was to immerse it in bleaching liquids, after which it was hung out to dry. Fumes from a manufacturer of sulphate of ammonia had the effect of turning the matting from a bright to a dull and blackish color. The reason for this was that the bleaching liquid contained chloride of tin, which, when affected by sulphuretted hydrogen, is turned to a darker color. An injunction was sought to stop the manufacturer from emitting the fumes. The lawyers for the defendant argued that if the plaintiff "were not to use . . . a particular bleaching liquid, their fibre would not be affected; that their process is unusual, not according to the custom of the trade, and even damaging to their own fabrics." The judge commented: ". . . it appears to me quite plain that a person has a right to carry on upon his own property a manufacturing process in which he uses chloride of tin, or any sort of metallic dye, and that his neighbour is not at liberty to pour in gas which will interfere with his manufacture. If it can be traced to the neighbour, then, I ap-

10. Cooke v. Forbes, 5 L.R.-Eq. 166 (1867–1868).

prehend, clearly he will have a right to come here and ask for relief." But in view of the fact that the damage was accidental and occasional, that careful precautions were taken, and that there was no exceptional risk, an injunction was refused, leaving the plaintiff to bring an action for damages if he wished. What the subsequent developments were I do not know. But it is clear that the situation is essentially the same as that found in *Sturges v. Bridgman,* except that the cocoa-nut fibre matting manufacturer could not secure an injunction but would have to seek damages from the sulphate of ammonia manufacturer. The economic analysis of the situation is exactly the same as with the cattle which destroyed crops. To avoid the damage, the sulphate of ammonia manufacturer could increase his precautions or move to another location. Either course would presumably increase his costs. Alternatively he could pay for the damage. This he would do if the payments for damage were less than the additional costs that would have to be incurred to avoid the damage. The payments for damage would then become part of the cost of production of sulphate of ammonia. Of course, if, as was suggested in the legal proceedings, the amount of damage could be eliminated by changing the bleaching agent (which would presumably increase the costs of the matting manufacturer) and if the additional cost was less than the damage that would otherwise occur, it should be possible for the two manufacturers to make a mutually satisfactory bargain whereby the new bleaching agent was used. Had the court decided against the matting manufacturer, as a consequence of which he would have had to suffer the damage without compensation, the allocation of resources would not have been affected. It would pay the matting manufacturer to change his bleaching agent if the additional cost involved was less than the reduction in damage. And since the matting manufacturer would be willing to pay the sulphate of ammonia manufacturer an amount up to his loss of income (the increase in costs or the damage suffered) if he would cease his activities, this loss of income would remain a cost of production for the manufacturer of sulphate of ammonia. This case is indeed analytically the same as the cattle example.

Bryant v. Lefever[11] raised the problem of the smoke nuisance in a novel form. The plaintiff and the defendants were occupiers of adjoining houses, which were of about the same height.

> Before 1876 the plaintiff was able to light a fire in any room of his house without the chimneys smoking; the two houses had remained in the same condition some thirty or forty years. In 1876 the defendants took down their house, and began to rebuild it. They carried up a wall by the side of the plaintiff's chimneys much beyond its original height, and stacked timber on the roof of their house, and thereby caused the plaintiff's chimneys to smoke whenever he lighted fires.

The reason, of course, why the chimneys smoked was that the erection of the wall and the stacking of the timber prevented the free circulation of air. In a trial before a jury, the plaintiff was awarded damages of £40. The case then went to the Court of Appeals, where the judgment was reversed. Bramwell, L. J., argued:

> . . . it is said, and the jury have found that the defendants have done that which caused a nuisance, but it is not of the defendants' causing. They have done nothing in causing the nuisance. Their house and their timber are harmless enough. It is the plaintiff who causes the nuisance by lighting a coal fire in a place the chimney of which is placed so near the defendants' wall, that the smoke does not escape, but comes into the house. Let the plaintiff cease to light his fire, let him move his chimney, let him carry it higher, and there would be no nuisance. Who then, causes it? It would be very clear that the plaintiff did, if he had built his house or chimney after the defendants had put the timber on theirs, and it is really the same though he did so before the timber was there. But (what is in truth the same answer), if the defendants cause the

11. Bryant v. Lefever, 4 C.P.D. 172 (1878–1879).

nuisance, they have a right to do so. If the plaintiff has not the right to the passage of air, except subject to the defendants' right to build or put timber on their house, then his right is subject to their right, and though a nuisance follows from the exercise of their right, they are not liable.

And Cotton, L. J., said:

Here it is found that the erection of the defendants' wall has sensibly and materially interfered with the comfort of human existence in the plaintiff's house, and it is said this is a nuisance for which the defendants are liable. Ordinarily this is so, but the defendants have done so, not by sending on to the plaintiff's property any smoke or noxious vapour, but by interrupting the egress of smoke from the plaintiff's house in a way to which . . . the plaintiff has no legal right. The plaintiff creates the smoke, which interferes with his comfort. Unless he has . . . a right to get rid of this in a particular way which has been interfered with by the defendants, he cannot sue the defendants, because the smoke made by himself, for which he has not provided any effectual means of escape, causes him annoyance. It is as if a man tried to get rid of liquid filth arising on his own land by a drain into his neighbour's land. Until a right had been acquired by user, the neighbour might stop the drain without incurring liability by so doing. No doubt great inconvenience would be caused to the owner of the property on which the liquid filth arises. But the act of his neighbour would be a lawful act, and he would not be liable for the consequences attributable to the fact that the man had accumulated filth without providing any effectual means of getting rid of it.

I do not propose to show that any subsequent modification of the situation, as a result of bargains between the parties (conditioned by the cost of stacking the timber elsewhere, the cost of extending the chimney higher, etc.), would have exactly the same result whatever decision the courts had come to, since this point has already been adequately dealt with in the discussion of the cattle example and the two previous cases. What I shall discuss is the argument of the judges in the Court of Appeals that the smoke nuisance was not caused by the man who erected the wall but by the man who lit the fires. The novelty of the situation is that the smoke nuisance was suffered by the man who lit the fires and not by some third person. The question is not a trivial one, since it lies at the heart of the problem under discussion. Who caused the smoke nuisance? The answer seems fairly clear. The smoke nuisance was caused both by the man who built the wall *and* by the man who lit the fires. Given the fires, there would have been no smoke nuisance without the wall; given the wall, there would have been no smoke nuisance without the fires. Eliminate the wall or the fires and the smoke nuisance would disappear. On the marginal principle it is clear that *both* were responsible and *both* should be forced to include the loss of amenity due to the smoke as a cost in deciding whether to continue the activity which gives rise to the smoke. And given the possibility of market transactions, this is what would in fact happen. Although the wall-builder was not liable legally for the nuisance, as the man with the smoking chimneys would presumably be willing to pay a sum equal to the monetary worth to him of eliminating the smoke, this sum would therefore become for the wall-builder a cost of continuing to have the high wall with the timber stacked on the roof.

The judges' contention that it was the man lighting the fires who alone caused the smoke nuisance is true only if we assume that the wall is the given factor. This is what the judges did by deciding that the man who erected the higher wall had a legal right to do so. The case would have been even more interesting if the smoke from the chimneys had injured the timber. Then it would have been the wall-builder who suffered the damage. The case would then have closely paralleled *Sturges v. Bridgman* and there can be little doubt that the man who lit the fires would have been liable for the ensuing damage to the timber, in spite of the fact that no damage had occurred until the high wall was built by the man who owned the timber.

Judges have to decide on legal liability, but this should not confuse economists about the nature of the economic problem involved. In the case of the cattle and the crops, it is true that there would be no crop damage without the cattle. It is equally true that there would be no crop damage without the crops. The doctor's work would not have been disturbed if the confectioner had not worked his machinery; but the machinery would have disturbd no one if the doctor had not set up his consulting room in that particular place. The matting was blackened by the fumes from the sulphate of ammonia manufacturer; but no damage would have occurred if the matting manufacturer had not chosen to hang out his matting in a particular place and to use a particular bleaching agent. If we are to discuss the problem in terms of causation, both parties cause the damage. If we are to attain an optimum allocation of resources, it is therefore desirable that both parties should take the harmful effect (the nuisance) into account in deciding on their course of action. It is one of the beauties of a smoothly operating pricing system that, as has already been explained, the fall in the value of production due to the harmful effect would be a cost for both parties.

Bass v. Gregory[12] will serve as an excellent final illustration of the problem. The plaintiffs were the owners and tenant of a public house called the Jolly Anglers. The defendant was the owner of some cottages and a yard adjoining the Jolly Anglers. Under the public house was a cellar excavated in the rock. From the cellar, a hole or shaft had been cut into an old well situated in the defendant's yard. The well therefore became the ventilating shaft for the cellar. The cellar "had been used for a particular purpose in the process of brewing, which, without ventilation, could not be carried on." The cause of the action was that the defendant removed a grating from the mouth of the well, "so as to stop or prevent the free passage of air from [the] cellar upwards through the well. . . ." What caused the defendant to take the step is not clear from the report of the case. Perhaps "the air . . . impregnated by the brewing operations" which "passed up the well and out into the open

---

12. Bass v. Gregory, 25 Q.B.D. 481 (1890).

air" was offensive to him. At any rate, he preferred to have the well in his yard stopped up. The court had first to determine whether the owners of the public house could have a legal right to a current of air. If they were to have such a right, this case would have to be distinguished from *Bryant v. Lefever* (already considered). This, however, presented no difficulty. In this case, the current of air was confined to "a strictly defined channel." In the case of *Bryant v. Lefever,* what was involved was "the general current of air common to all mankind." The judge therefore held that the owners of the public house could have the right to a current of air, whereas the owner of the private house in *Bryant v. Lefever* could not. An economist might be tempted to add "but the air moved all the same." However, all that had been decided at this stage of the argument was that there could be a legal right, not that the owners of the public house possessed it. But evidence showed that the shaft from the cellar to the well had existed for over forty years and that the use of the well as a ventilating shaft must have been known to the owners of the yard, since the air, when it emerged, smelt of the brewing operations. The judge therefore held that the public house had such a right by the "doctrine of lost grant." This doctrine states "that if a legal right is proved to have existed and been exercised for a number of years the law ought to presume that it had a legal origin."[13] So the owner of the cottages and yard had to unstop the well and endure the smell.

---

13. It may be asked why a lost grant could not also be presumed in the case of the confectioner who had operated one mortar for more than sixty years. The answer is that until the doctor built the consulting room at the end of his garden there was no nuisance. So the nuisance had not continued for many years. It is true that the confectioner in his affidavit referred to "an invalid lady who occupied the house upon one occasion, about thirty years before" who "requested him if possible to discontinue the use of the mortars before eight o'clock in the morning" and that there was some evidence that the garden wall had been subjected to vibration. But the court had little difficulty in disposing of this line of argument: ". . . this vibration, even if it existed at all, was so slight, and the complaint, if it can be called a complaint, of the invalid lady . . . was of so trifling a character, that . . . the Defendant's acts would not have given rise to any proceeding either at law or in equity" (11 Ch.D. 863). That is, the confectioner had not committed a nuisance until the doctor built his consulting room.

The reasoning employed by the courts in determining legal rights will often seem strange to an economist, because many of the factors on which the decision turns are, to an economist, irrelevant. Because of this, situations which are, from an economic point of view, identical will be treated quite differently by the courts. The economic problem in all cases of harmful effects is how to maximize the value of production. In the case of *Bass v. Gregory,* fresh air was drawn in through the well to facilitate the production of beer, but foul air was expelled through the well, making life in the adjoining houses less pleasant. The economic problem was to decide which to choose: a lower cost of beer and worsened amenities in adjoining houses, or a higher cost of beer and improved amenities. In deciding this question, the ''doctrine of lost grant'' is about as relevant as the colour of the judge's eyes. But it has to be remembered that the immediate question faced by the courts is *not* what shall be done by whom *but* who has the legal right to do what. It is always possible to modify by transactions on the market the initial legal delimitation of rights. And, of course, if such market transactions are costless, such a rearrangment of rights will always take place if it would lead to an increase in the value of production.

VI. The Cost of Market Transactions Taken into Account

The argument has proceeded up to this point on the assumption (explicit in sections III and IV and tacit in section V) that there were no costs involved in carrying out market transactions. This is, of course, a very unrealistic assumption. In order to carry out a market transaction, it is necessary to discover who it is that one wishes to deal with, to inform people that one wishes to deal and on what terms, to conduct negotiations leading up to a bargain, to draw up the contract, to undertake the inspection needed to make sure that the terms of the contract are being observed, and so on. These operations are often extremely costly, sufficiently costly at any rate to prevent many transactions that would be carried out in a world in which the pricing system worked without cost.

In earlier sections, when dealing with the problem of the rearrangement of legal rights through the market, I argued that such a rearrangement would be made through the market whenever this would lead to an increase in the value of production. But this assumed costless market transactions. Once the costs of carrying out market transactions are taken into account, it is clear that such a rearrangement of rights will only be undertaken when the increase in the value of production consequent upon the rearrangement is greater than the costs which would be involved in bringing it about. When it is less, the granting of an injunction (or the knowledge that it would be granted) or the liability to pay damages may result in an activity being discontinued (or may prevent its being started) which would be undertaken if market transactions were costless. In these conditions, the initial delimitation of legal rights does have an effect on the efficiency with which the economic system operates. One arrangement of rights may bring about a greater value of production than any other. But unless this is the arrangement of rights established by the legal system, the costs of reaching the same result by altering and combining rights through the market may be so great that this optimal arrangement of rights, and the greater value of production which it would bring, may never be achieved. The part played by economic considerations in the process of delimiting legal rights will be discussed in the next section. In this section, I will take the initial delimitation of rights and the costs of carrying out market transactions as given.

It is clear that an alternative form of economic organization which could achieve the same result at less cost than would be incurred by using the market would enable the value of production to be raised. As I explained many years ago, the firm represents such an alternative to organizing production through market transactions.[14] Within the firm, individual bargains between the various co-operating factors of production are eliminated and for a market transaction is substituted an administrative decision. The rearrangement of production then takes place without the need for bargains among the owners

14. See "The Nature of the Firm," 33–55.

of the factors of production. A landowner who has control of a large tract of land may devote his land to various uses, taking into account the effect that the interrelations of the various activities will have on the net return of the land, thus rendering unnecessary bargains between those undertaking the various activities. Owners of a large building or of several adjoining properties in a given area may act in much the same way. In effect, based upon our earlier terminology, the firm would acquire the legal rights of all the parties, and the rearrangement of activities would not follow on a rearrangement of rights by contract but as a result of an administrative decision as to how the rights should be used.

It does not, of course, follow that the administrative costs of organizing a transaction through a firm are inevitably less than the costs of the market transactions which are superseded. But where contracts are peculiarly difficult to draw up and an attempt to describe what the parties have agreed to do or not to do (for example, the amount and kind of a smell or noise that they may make or will not make) would necessitate a lengthy and highly involved document, and where, as is probable, a long-term contract would be desirable,[15] it would be hardly surprising if the emergence of a firm or the extension of the activities of an existing firm was not the solution adopted on many occasions to deal with the problem of harmful effects. This solution would be adopted whenever the administrative costs of the firm were less than the costs of the market transactions that it supersedes and the gains which would result from the rearrangement of activities greater than the firm's costs of organizing them. I do not need to examine in great detail the character of this solution since I have explained what is involved in my earlier article.

But the firm is not the only possible answer to this problem. The administrative costs of organizing transactions within the firm may also be high, and particularly so when many diverse activities are brought within the control of a single organization. In the standard case of a smoke nuisance, which may

15. For reasons explained in my earlier article, see "The Nature of the Firm," 39.

affect a vast number of people engaged in a wide variety of activities, the administrative costs might well be so high as to make any attempt to deal with the problem within the confines of a single firm impossible. An alternative solution is direct governmental regulation. Instead of instituting a legal system of rights which can be modified by transactions on the market, the government may impose regulations which state what people must or must not do and which have to be obeyed. Thus, the government (by statute or perhaps more likely through an administrative agency) may, to deal with the problem of smoke nuisance, decree that certain methods of production should or should not be used (for example, that smoke-preventing devices should be installed or that coal or oil should not be burned) or may confine certain types of business to certain districts (zoning regulations).

The government is, in a sense, a super-firm (but of a very special kind) since it is able to influence the use of factors of productions by administrative decision. But the ordinary firm is subject to checks in its operations because of the competition of other firms which might administer the same activities at lower cost, and also because there is always the alternative of market transactions against organization within the firm if the administrative costs become too great. The government is able, if it wishes, to avoid the market altogether, which a firm can never do. The firm has to make market agreements with the owners of the factors of production that it uses. Just as the government can conscript or seize property, so it can decree that factors of production should only be used in such-and-such a way. Such authoritarian methods save a lot of trouble (for those doing the organizing). Furthermore, the government has at its disposal the police and the other law enforcement agencies to make sure that its regulations are carried out.

It is clear that the government has powers which might enable it to get some things done at a lower cost than could a private organization (or at any rate one without special governmental powers). But the governmental administrative machine is not itself costless. It can, in fact, on occasion be extremely costly. Furthermore, there is no reason to suppose that the restrictive and zoning regulations, made by a fallible administration subject to political pressures and operating without any competitive check, will necessarily always be those which increase the efficiency with which the economic system operates. Furthermore, such general regulations which must apply to a wide variety of cases will be enforced in some cases in which they are clearly inappropriate. From these considerations it follows that direct governmental regulations will not necessarily give better results than leaving the problem to be solved by the market or the firm. But equally, there is no reason why, on occasion, such governmental administrative regulation should not lead to an improvement in economic efficiency. This would seem particularly likely when, as is normally the case with the smoke nuisance, a large number of people is involved and when therefore the costs of handling the problem through the market or the firm may be high.

There is, of course, a further alternative, which is to do nothing about the problem at all. And given that the costs involved in solving the problem by regulations issued by the governmental administrative machine will often be heavy (particularly if the costs are interpreted to include all the consequences which follow from the government engaging in this kind of activity), it will no doubt be commonly the case that the gain which would come from regulating the actions which give rise to the harmful effects will be less than the costs involved in governmental regulation.

The discussion of the problem of harmful effects in this section (when the costs of market transactions are taken into account) is extremely inadequate. But at least it has made clear that the problem is one of choosing the appropriate social arrangement for dealing with the harmful effects. All solutions have costs, and there is no reason to suppose that governmental regulation is called for simply because the problem is not well handled by the market or the firm. Satisfactory views on policy can only come from a patient study of how, in practice, the market, firms, and governments handle the problem of harmful effects. Economists need to study the work of the broker in bringing parties together, the effectiveness of restrictive covenants, the problems of the large-scale real-estate development company, the operation of governmental zoning, and other regulating activities. It is my belief that economists, and policy-makers generally, have tended to over-estimate the advantages which come from governmental regulation. But this belief, even if justified, does not do more than suggest that governmental regulation should be curtailed. It does not tell us where the boundary line should be drawn. This, it seems to me, has to come from a detailed investigation of the actual results of handling the problem in different ways. But it would be unfortunate if this investigation were undertaken with the aid of a faulty economic analysis. The aim of this article is to indicate what the economic approach to the problem should be.

VII. The Legal Delimitation of Rights and the Economic Problem

The discussion in section V not only served to illustrate the argument but also afforded a glimpse at the legal approach to the problem of harmful effects. The cases considered were all English, but a similar selection of American cases could easily be made and the character of the reasoning would have been the same. Of course, if market transactions were costless, all that matters (questions of equity apart) is that the rights of the various parties should be well defined and the results of legal actions easy to forecast. But as we have seen, the situation is quite different when market transactions are so costly as to make it difficult to change the arrangement of rights established by the law. In such cases, the courts directly influence economic activity. It would therefore seem desirable that the courts should understand the economic consequence of their decisions and should, insofar as this is possible without creating too much uncertainty about the legal position itself, take these consequences into account when making their decisions. Even when it is possible to change the legal delimitation of rights through market transactions, it is obviously desirable to reduce the need for such transactions and thus reduce the employment of resources in carrying them out.

A thorough examination of the presuppositions of the courts in trying such cases would be of great interest, but I have not been able to attempt it. Nevertheless, it is clear from a cursory study that the courts have often recognized the economic implications of their decisions and are aware (as many economists are not) of the reciprocal nature of the problem. Furthermore, from time to time, they take these economic implications into account, along with other factors, in arriving at their decisions. The American writers on this subject refer to the question in a more explicit fashion than do the British. Thus, to quote *Prosser on Torts,* a person may

> make use of his own property or . . . conduct his own affairs at the expense of some harm to his neighbors. He may operate a factory whose noise and smoke cause some discomfort to others, so long as he keeps within reasonable bounds. It is only when his conduct is unreasonable, *in the light of its utility and the harm which results* [italics added], that it becomes a nuisance. . . . As it was said in an ancient case in regard to candlemaking in a town, "Le utility del chose excusera le noisomeness del stink."
>
> The world must have factories, smelters, oil refineries, noisy machinery and blasting, even at the expense of some inconvenience to those in the vicinity and the plaintiff may be required to accept some not unreasonable discomfort for the general good.[16]

The standard British writers do not state as explicitly as this that a comparison between the utility and harm produced is an element in deciding whether a harmful effect should be considered a nuisance. But similar views, if less strongly ex-

16. See William L. Prosser, *Handbook of the Law of Torts,* 2nd ed. (St. Paul, Minn.: West Publishing Co., 1955), 398–99, 412. The quotation about the ancient case concerning candle making is taken from Sir James Fitzjames Stephen, *A General View of the Criminal Law of England,* 2nd ed. (London: Macmillan & Co., 1890), 106. Sir James Stephen gives no reference. He perhaps had in mind *Rex. v. Ronkett,* included in Warren A. Seavey, Keeton, and Thurston, *Cases and Materials on the Law of Torts* (St. Paul, Minn.: West Publishing Co., 1950), 604. A similar view to that expressed by Prosser is to be found in Fowler V. Harper and Fleming James, Jr., *The Law of Torts,* 2nd ed. (Boston: Little, Brown, 1956), 67–74; Restatement, Torts §§826, 827, and 828.

pressed, are to be found.[17] The doctrine that the harmful effect must be substantial before the court will act is, no doubt, in part a reflection of the fact that there will almost always be some gain to offset the harm. And in the reports of individual cases, it is clear that the judges have had in mind what would be lost as well as what would be gained in deciding whether to grant an injunction or award damages. Thus, in refusing to prevent the destruction of a prospect by a new building, the judge stated:

> I know no general rule of common law, which . . . says, that building so as to stop another's prospect is a nuisance. Was that the case, there could be no great towns; and I must grant injunctions to all the new buildings in the town.[18]

In *Webb v. Bird*[19] it was decided that it was not a nuisance to build a schoolhouse so near a windmill as to obstruct currents of air and hinder the working of the mill. An early case seems to have been decided in an opposite direction. Gale commented:

> In old maps of London a row of windmills appears on the heights to the north of London. Probably in the time of King James it was thought an alarming circumstance, as affecting the supply of food to the city, that anyone should build so near them as to take the wind out from their sails.[20]

17. See Sir Percy H. Winfield, *Winfield on Torts,* 6th ed. by T. E. Lewis (London: Sweet & Maxwell, 1954); John W. Salmond, *Salmond on the Law of Torts,* 12th ed. by R. F. V. Heuston (London: Sweet & Maxwell, 1957), 181–90; Harry Street, *The Law of Torts,* 2nd ed. (London: Butterworth, 1959), 221–29.

18. Attorney General v. Doughty, 2 Ves. Se. 453, 28 Eng. Rep. 290 (Ch. 1752). Compare in this connection the statement of an American judge, quoted in Prosser, *Law of Torts,* 413, n. 54: "Without smoke, Pittsburgh would have remained a very pretty village," Musmanno, J., in Versailles Borough v. McKessport Coal & Coke Co., 83 Pitts. Leg. J. 379,385, 1935.

19. Webb v. Bird, 10 C.B. (N.S.) 268, 142 Eng. Rep. 445 (1861); 13 C.B. (N.S.) 841, 143 Eng. Rep. 332 (1863).

20. See *Gale on Easements,* 238, n. 6.

In one of the cases discussed in section V, *Sturges v. Bridgman,* it seems clear that the judges were thinking of the economic consequences of alternative decisions. To the argument that if the principle that they seemed to be following

> were carried out to its logical consequences, it would result in the most serious practical inconvenience, for a man might go—say into a midst of the tanneries of Bermondsey, or into any other locality devoted to any particular trade or manufacture of a noisy or unsavoury character, and by building a private residence upon a vacant piece of land put a stop to such trade or manufacture altogether,

the judges answered that

> whether anything is a nuisance or not is a question to be determined, not merely by an abstract consideration of the thing itself, but in reference to its circumstances; what would be a nuisance in *Belgrave Square* would not necessarily be so in *Bermondsey;* and where a locality is devoted to a particular trade or manufacture carried on by the traders or manufacturers in a particular and established manner not constituting a public nuisance, Judges and juries would be justified in finding, and may be trusted to find, that the trade or manufacture so carried on in that locality is not a private or actionable wrong.[21]

That the character of the neighbourhood is relevant in deciding whether something is, or is not, a nuisance, is definitely established.

> He who dislikes the noise of traffic must not set up his abode in the heart of a great city. He who loves peace and quiet must not live in a locality devoted to the business of making boilers or steamships.[22]

21. 11 Ch. D. 865 (1879).
22. Salmond, *Law of Torts,* 182.

What has emerged has been described as "planning and zoning by the judiciary."[23] Of course there are sometimes considerable difficulties in applying the criteria.[24]

An interesting example of the problem is found in *Adams v. Ursell*,[25] in which a fried fish shop in a predominantly working-class district was set up near houses of "a much better character." England without fish-and-chips is a contradiction in terms and the case was clearly one of high importance. The judge commented:

> It was urged that an injunction would cause great hardship to the defendant and to the poor people who get food at his shop. The answer to that is that it does not follow that the defendant cannot carry on his business in another more suitable place somewhere in the neighbourhood. It by no means follows that because a fried fish shop is a nuisance in one place it is a nuisance in another.

In fact, the injunction which restrained Ursell from running his shop did not even extend to the whole street. So he was presumably able to move to other premises near houses of "a much worse character," the inhabitants of which would no doubt consider the availability of fish-and-chips to out-weigh the pervading odour and "fog or mist" so graphically described by the plaintiff. Had there been no other "more suitable place in the neighbourhood," the case would have been more difficult and the decision might have been different. What would "the poor people" have had for food? No English judge would have said: "Let them eat cake."

The courts do not always refer very clearly to the economic problem posed by the cases brought before them, but it seems probable that in the interpretation of words and phrases like "reasonable" or "common or ordinary use" there is some

23. Charles M. Haar, *Land-Use Planning, A Casebook on the Use, Misuse, and Re-use of Urban Land* (Boston: Little, Brown, 1959), 95.

24. See, for example, Rushmer v. Polsue and Alfieri, Ltd. [1906] 1 Ch. 234, which deals with the case of a house in a quiet situation in a noisy district.

25. Adams v. Ursell, [1913] 1 Ch. 269.

recognition, perhaps largely unconscious and certainly not very explicit, of the economic aspects of the question at issue. A good example of this would seem to be the judgment in the Court of Appeals in *Andreae v. Selfridge and Company Ltd.*[26] In this case, a hotel (in Wigmore Street) was situated on part of an island site. The remainder of the site was acquired by Selfridges, which demolished the existing buildings in order to erect another in their place. The hotel suffered a loss of custom in consequence of the noise and dust caused by the demolition. The owner of the hotel brought an action against Selfridges for damages. In the lower court, the hotel was awarded £4,500 damages. The case was then taken on appeal.

The judge who had found for the hotel proprietor in the lower court said:

> I cannot regard what the defendants did on the site of the first operation as having been commonly done in the ordinary use and occupation of land or houses. It is neither usual nor common, in this country, for people to excavate a site to a depth of 60 feet and then to erect upon that site a steel framework and fasten the steel frames together with rivets. . . . Nor is it, I think, a common or ordinary use of land, in this country, to act as the defendants did when they were dealing with the site of their second operation—namely, to demolish all the houses that they had to demolish, five or six of them I think, if not more, and to use for the purpose of demolishing them pneumatic hammers.

Sir Wilfred Green, M. R., speaking for the Court of Appeals, first noted

> that when one is dealing with temporary operations, such as demolition and re-building, everybody has to put up with a certain amount of discomfort, because operations of that kind cannot be carried on at all without a certain amount of noise and a certain amount of dust. Therefore, the rule with regard to interference must be read subject to this qualification.

26. Andreae v. Selfridge and Company Ltd., [1938] 1 Ch. 1.

He then referred to the previous judgment:

> With great respect to the learned judge, I take the view
> that he has not approached this matter from the correct
> angle. It seems to me that it is not possible to say . . .
> that the type of demolition, excavation and construc-
> tion in which the defendant company was engaged in
> the course of these operations was of such an abnormal
> and unusual nature as to prevent the qualification to
> which I have referred coming into operation. It seems
> to me that, when the rule speaks of the common or
> ordinary use of land, it does not mean that the methods
> of using land and building on it are in some way to be
> established for ever. As time goes on new inventions
> or new methods enable land to be more profitably used,
> either by digging down into the earth or by mounting
> up into the skies. Whether, from other points of view,
> that is a matter which is desirable for humanity is nei-
> ther here nor there; but it is part of the normal use of
> land, to make use upon your land, in the matter of
> construction, of what particular type and what partic-
> ular depth of foundations and particular height of build-
> ing may be reasonable, in the circumstances, and in
> view of the developments of the day. . . . Guests at
> hotels are very easily upset. People coming to this
> hotel, who were accustomed to a quiet outlook at the
> back, coming back and finding demolition and building
> going on, may very well have taken the view that the
> particular merit of this hotel no longer existed. That
> would be a misfortune for the plaintiff; but assuming
> that there was nothing wrong in the defendant com-
> pany's works, assuming the defendant company was
> carrying on the demolition and its building, productive
> of noise though it might be, with all reasonable skill,
> and taking all reasonable precautions not to cause an-
> noyance to its neighbours, then the plaintiff might lose
> all her clients in the hotel because they have lost the
> amenities of an open and quiet place behind, but she
> would have no cause of complaint. . . [But those] who
> say that their interference with the comfort of their
> neighbours is justified because their operations are nor-
> mal and usual and conducted with proper care and skill

are under a specific duty . . . to use that reasonable and proper care and skill. It is not a correct attitude to take to say: "We will go on and do what we like until somebody complains!" . . . Their duty is to take proper precautions and to see that the nuisance is reduced to a minimum. It is no answer for them to say: "But this would mean that we should have to do the work more slowly than we would like to do it, or it would involve putting us to some extra expense." All these questions are matters of common sense and degree, and quite clearly it would be unreasonable to expect people to conduct their work so slowly or so expensively, for the purpose of preventing a transient inconvenience, that the cost and trouble would be prohibitive. . . . In this case, the defendant company's attitude seems to have been to go on until somebody complained, and, further, that its desire to hurry its work and conduct it according to its own ideas and its own convenience was to prevail if there was a real conflict between it and the comfort of its neighbours. That . . . is not carrying out the obligations of using reasonable care and skill. . . . The effect comes to this . . . the plaintiff suffered an actionable nuisance; . . . she is entitled, not to a nominal sum, but to a substantial sum, based upon those principles . . . but in arriving at the sum . . . I have discounted any loss of custom . . . which might be due to the general loss of amenities owing to what was going on at the back. . . .

The upshot was that the damages awarded were reduced from £4,500 to £1,000.

The discussion in this section has, up to this point, been concerned with court decisions arising out of the common law relating to nuisance. Delimitation of rights in this area also comes about because of statutory enactments. Most economists would appear to assume that the aim of governmental action in this field is to extend the scope of the law of nuisance by designating as nuisances activities which would not be recognized as such by the common law. And there can be no doubt that some statutes, for example, the Public Health Acts, have had this effect. But not all governmental enactments are of this kind. The effect of much of the legislation in this area is to protect businesses from the claims of those they have harmed by their actions. There is a long list of legalized nuisances.

The position has been summarized in *Halsbury's Laws of England* as follows:

> Where the legislature directs that a thing shall in all events be done or authorises certain works at a particular place for a specific purpose or grants powers with the intention that they shall be exercised, although leaving some discretion as to the mode of exercise, no action will lie at common law for nuisance or damage which is the inevitable result of carrying out the statutory powers so conferred. This is so whether the act causing the damage is authorised for public purposes or private profit. Acts done under powers granted by persons to whom Parliament has delegated authority to grant such powers, for example, under provisional orders of the Board of Trade, are regarded as having been done under statutory authority. In the absence of negligence it seems that a body exercising statutory powers will not be liable for an action merely because it might, by acting in a different way, have minimised an injury.

Instances are next given of freedom from liability for acts authorized:

> An action has been held not to be against a body exercising its statutory powers without negligence in respect of the flooding of land by water escaping from water-courses, from water pipes, from drains, or from a canal; the escape of fumes from sewers; the escape of sewage; the subsidence of a road over a sewer; vibration or noise caused by a railway; fires caused by authorized acts; the pollution of a stream where statutory requirements to use the best known method of purifying before discharging the effluent have been satisfied; interference with a telephone or telegraph system by an electric tramway; the insertion of poles for tramways in the subsoil; annoyance caused by things

reasonably necessary for the excavation of authorised works; accidental damage caused by the placing of a grating in a roadway; the escape of tar acid; or interference with the access of a frontager by a street shelter or safety railings on the edge of a pavement.[27]

The legal position in the United States would seem to be essentially the same as in England, except that the power of the legislature to authorize what would otherwise be nuisances under the common law, at least without giving compensation to the person harmed, is somewhat more limited, as it is subject to constitutional restrictions.[28] Nonetheless, the power is there and cases more or less identical with the English cases can be found. The question has arisen in an acute form in connection with airports and the operation of aeroplanes. The case of *Delta Air Corporation v. Kersey, Kersey v. City of Atlanta*[29] is a good example. Kersey bought land and built a house on it. Some years later the City of Atlanta constructed an airport on land immediately adjoining that of Kersey. It was explained that his property was "a quiet, peaceful and proper location for a home before the airport was built, but dust, noises and low flying of airplanes caused by the operation of the airport have rendered his property unsuitable as a home," a state of affairs which was described in the report of the case with a wealth of distressing detail. The judge first referred to an earlier case, *Thrasher v. City of Atlanta*,[30] in which it was noted that the City of Atlanta had been expressly authorized to operate an airport.

By this franchise aviation was recognized as a lawful business and also as an enterprise affected with a public

---

27. John Anthony Hardinge Giffard, 3rd Earl of Halsbury, ed., "Public Authorities and Public Officers," *Halsbury's Laws of England*, vol. 30, 3rd ed. (London: Butterworth, 1960), 690–91.

28. See Prosser, *Law of Torts*, 421; Harper and James, *Law of Torts*, 86–87.

29. Delta Air Corporation v. Kersey, Kersey v. City of Atlanta, Supreme Court of Georgia, 193 Ga. 862, 20 S.E. 2d 245 (1942).

30. Thrasher v. City of Atlanta, 178 Ga. 514, 173 S.E. 817 (1934).

interest . . . all persons using [the airport] in the manner contemplated by law are within the protection and immunity of the franchise granted by the municipality. An airport is not a nuisance per se, although it might become such from the manner of its construction or operation.

Since aviation was a lawful business affected with a public interest and the construction of the airport was authorized by statute, the judge next referred to *Georgia Railroad and Banking Co. v. Maddox*[31] in which it was said:

Where a railroad terminal yard is located and its construction authorized, under statutory powers, if it be constructed and operated in a proper manner, it cannot be adjudged a nuisance. Accordingly, injuries and inconveniences to persons residing near such a yard, from noises of locomotives, rumbling of cars, vibrations produced thereby, and smoke, cinders, soot and the like, which result from the ordinary and necessary, therefore proper, use and operation of such a yard, are not nuisances, but are the necessary concomitants of the franchise granted.

In view of this, the judge decided that the noise and dust complained of by Mr. Kersey "may be deemed to be incidental to the proper operation of an airport, and as such they cannot be said to constitute a nuisance." But the complaint against low flying was different:

. . . can it be said that flights . . . at such low height [25 to 50 feet above Mr. Kersey's house] as to be imminently dangerous to . . . life and health . . . are a necessary concomitant of an airport? We do not think this question can be answered in the affirmative. No reason appears why the city could not obtain lands of an area [sufficiently large] . . . as not to require such low flights. . . . For the sake of public convenience

31. Georgia Railroad and Banking Co. v. Maddox, 116 Ga. 64, 42 S.E. 315 (1902).

adjoining-property owners must suffer such inconvenience from noise and dust as result from the usual and proper operation of an airport, but their private rights are entitled to preference in the eyes of the law where the inconvenience is not one demanded by a properly constructed and operated airport.

Of course this is assumed that the City of Atlanta could prevent the low flying and continue to operate the airport. The judge therefore added:

From all it appears, the conditions causing the low flying may be remedied; but if on the trial it should appear that it is indispensable to the public interest that the airport should continue to be operated in its present condition, it may be said that the petitioner should be denied injunctive relief.

In the course of another aviation case, *Smith v. New England Aircraft Co.,*[32] the court surveyed the law in the United States regarding the legalizing of nuisances and it is apparent that, in the broad, it is very similar to that found in England:

It is the proper function of the legislative department of government in the exercise of the police power to consider the problems and risks that arise from the use of new inventions and endeavor to adjust private rights and harmonize conflicting interests by comprehensive statutes for the public welfare . . . There are . . . analogies where the invasion of the airspace over underlying land by noise, smoke, vibration, dust and disagreeable odors, having been authorized by the legislative department of government and not being in effect a condemnation of the property although in some measure depreciating its market value, must be borne by the landowner without compensation or remedy. Legislative sanction makes that lawful which otherwise might be a nuisance. Examples of this are damages to

32. Smith v. New England Aircraft Co. 270 Mass. 511, 170 N.E. 385, 390 (1930).

adjacent land arising from smoke, vibration and noise
in the operation of a railroad . . . ; the noise of ringing
factory bells . . . ; the abatement of nuisances . . . ;
the erection of steam engines and furnaces . . . ; unpleasant odors connected with sewers, oil refining and
storage of naphtha. . . .

Most economists seem to be unaware of all this. When
they are prevented from sleeping at night by the roar of jet
planes overhead (publicly authorized and perhaps publicly operated), are unable to think (or rest) in the day because of the
noise and vibration from passing trains (publicly authorized
and perhaps publicly operated), find it difficult to breathe because of the odour from the local sewage farm (publicly authorized and perhaps publicly operated), and are unable to
escape because their driveways are blocked by a road obstruc-
tion (without any doubt, publicly devised), their nerves frayed
and mental balance disturbed, they proceed to declaim about
the disadvantages of private enterprise and the need for governmental regulation.

While most economists seem to be under a misapprehension concerning the character of the situation with which they
are dealing, it is also the case that the activities which they
would like to see stopped or curtailed may well be socially
justified. It is all a question of weighing up the gains that would
accrue from eliminating these harmful effects against the gains
that accrue from allowing them to continue. Of course, it is
likely that an extension of governmental economic activity will
often lead to this protection against action for nuisance being
pushed further than is desirable. For one thing, the government
is likely to look with a benevolent eye on enterprises which it
is itself promoting. For another, it is possible to describe the
committing of a nuisance by public enterprise in a much more
pleasant way than when the same thing is done by private
enterprise. In the words of Lord Justice Sir Alfred Denning:

. . . the significance of the social revolution of today
is that, whereas in the past the balance was much too
heavily in favour of the rights of property and freedom

of contract, Parliament has repeatedly intervened so as to give the public good its proper place.[33]

There can be little doubt that the Welfare State is likely to bring an extension of that immunity from liability for damage, which economists have been in the habit of condemning (although they have tended to assume that this immunity was a sign of too little governmental intervention in the economic system). For example, in Britain the powers of local authorities are regarded as being either absolute or conditional. In the first category, the local authority has no discretion in exercising the power conferred on it. "The absolute power may be said to cover all the necessary consequences of its direct operation even if such consequences amount to nuisance." On the other hand, a conditional power may only be exercised in such a way that the consequences do not constitute a nuisance.

> It is the intention of the legislature which determines whether a power is absolute or conditional. . . . [As] there is the possibility that the social policy of the legislature may change from time to time, a power which in one era would be construed as being conditional, might in another era be interpreted as being absolute in order to further the policy of the Welfare State. This point is one which should be borne in mind when considering some of the older cases upon this aspect of the law of nuisance.[34]

It would seem desirable to summarize the burden of this long section. The problem which we face in dealing with actions which have harmful effects is not simply one of restraining those responsible for them. What has to be decided is whether the gain from preventing the harm is greater than the loss which would be suffered elsewhere as a result of stopping the action which produced the harm. In a world in which there are costs of rearranging the rights established by the legal system, the

33. See Sir Alfred Denning, *Freedom Under the Law* (London: Stevens, 1949), 71.

34. Mary B. Cairns, *The Law of Tort in Local Government* (London: Shaw, 1954), 28–32.

courts, in cases relating to nuisance, are, in effect, making a decision on the economic problem and determining how resources are to be employed. It was argued that the courts are conscious of this and that they often make, although not always in a very explicit fashion, a comparison between what would be gained and what lost by preventing actions which have harmful effects. But the delimitation of rights is also the result of statutory enactments. Here we also find evidence of an appreciation of the reciprocal nature of the problem. While statutory enactments add to the list of nuisances, action is also taken to legalize what would otherwise be nuisances under the common law. The kind of situation which economists are prone to consider as requiring corrective governmental action is, in fact, often the result of governmental action. Such action is not necessarily unwise. But there is a real danger that extensive governmental intervention in the economic system may lead to the protection of those responsible for harmful effects being carried too far.

VIII. Pigou's Treatment in *The Economics of Welfare*

The fountainhead for the modern economic analysis of the problem discussed in this article is Pigou's *The Economics of Welfare* and, in particular, that section of Part II which deals with divergences between social and private net products which come about because

> one person A, in the course of rendering some service, for which payment is made, to a second person B, incidentally also renders services or disservices to other persons (not producers of like services), of such a sort that payment cannot be exacted from the benefited parties or compensation enforced on behalf of the injured parties.[35]

35. A. C. Pigou, *The Economics of Welfare,* 4th ed. (London: Macmillan & Co., 1932), 183. My references will all be to the fourth edition but the argument and examples examined in this article remained substantially unchanged from the first edition in 1920 to the fourth in 1932. A large part (but not all) of this analysis had appeared previously in *Wealth and Welfare* (London: Macmillan & Co., 1912).

Pigou tells us that his aim in Part II of *The Economics of Welfare* is

> to ascertain how far the free play of self-interest, acting under the existing legal system, tends to distribute the country's resources in the way most favorable to the production of a large national dividend, and how far it is feasible for State action to improve upon "natural" tendencies.[36]

If one is to judge from the first part of this statement, Pigou's purpose is to discover whether any improvements could be made in the existing arrangements which determine the use of resources. Since Pigou's conclusion is that improvements could be made, one might have expected him to continue by saying that he proposed to set out the changes required to bring them about. Instead, Pigou adds a phrase which contrasts "natural" tendencies with State action, which seems in some sense to equate the present arrangements with "natural" tendencies and to imply that what is required to bring about these improvements is State action (if feasible). That this is more or less Pigou's position is evident from chapter 1 of part II.[37] Pigou starts by referring to "optimistic followers of the classical economists"[38] who have argued that the value of production would be maximized if the government refrained from any interference in the economic system and the economic arrangements were those which came about "naturally." Pigou goes on to say that if self-interest does promote economic welfare, it is because human institutions have been devised to make it so. (This part of Pigou's argument, which he develops with the aid of a quotation from Cannan, seems to me to be essentially correct.) Pigou concludes:

36. Ibid.

37. Ibid., 127–30.

38. In *Wealth and Welfare*, Pigou attributes the "optimism" to Adam Smith himself and not to his followers. He there refers to the "highly optimistic theory of Adam Smith that the national dividend, in given circumstances of demand and supply, tends 'naturally' to a maximum" (p. 104).

> But even in the most advanced States there are failures
> and imperfections . . . there are many obstacles that
> prevent a community's resources from being distrib-
> uted . . . in the most efficient way. The study of these
> constitutes our present problem . . . its purpose is es-
> sentially practical. It seeks to bring into clearer light
> some of the ways in which it now is, or eventually may
> become, feasible for governments to control the play
> of economic forces in such wise as to promote the
> economic welfare, and through that, the total welfare,
> of their citizens as a whole.[39]

Pigou's underlying thought would appear to be: Some have
argued that no State action is needed. But the system has
performed as well as it has because of State action. Nonetheless, there are still imperfections. What additional State action
is required?

If this is a correct summary of Pigou's position, its inadequacy can be demonstrated by examining the first example
he gives of a divergence between private and social products.

> It might happen . . . that costs are thrown upon people
> not directly concerned, through, say, uncompensated
> damage done to surrounding woods by sparks from
> railway engines. All such effects must be included—
> some of them will be positive, others negative ele-
> ments—in reckoning up the social net product of the
> marginal increment of any volume of resources turned
> into any use or place.[40]

The example used by Pigou refers to a real situation. In Britain,
a railway does not normally have to compensate those who
suffer damage by fire caused by sparks from an engine. In
conjunction with what he says in chapter 9 of part II, I take
Pigou's policy recommendations to be, first, that there should
be State action to correct this "natural" situation, and second,
that the railways should be forced to compensate those whose

39. Pigou, *Economics of Welfare*, 129–30.
40. Ibid., 134.

woods are burnt. If this is a correct interpretation of Pigou's position, I would argue that the first recommendation is based on the misapprehension of the facts and that the second is not necessarily desirable.

Let us consider the legal position. Under the heading "Sparks from engines," we find the following in *Halsbury's Laws of England:*

> If railway undertakers use steam engines on their railway without express statutory authority to do so, they are liable, irrespective of any negligence on their part, for fires caused by sparks from engines. Railway undertakers are, however, generally given statutory authority to use steam engines on their railway; accordingly, if an engine is constructed with the precautions which science suggests against fire and is used without negligence, they are not responsible at common law for any damage which may be done by sparks. . . . In the construction of an engine the undertaker is bound to use all the discoveries which science has put within its reach in order to avoid doing harm, provided they are such as it is reasonable to require the company to adopt, having proper regard to the likelihood of the damage and to the cost and convenience of the remedy; but it is not negligence on the part of an undertaker if it refuses to use an apparatus the efficiency of which is open to bona fide doubt.

To this general rule, there is a statutory exception arising from the Railway (Fires) Act, 1905, as amended in 1923. This concerns agricultural land or agricultural crops.

> In such a case the fact that the engine was used under statutory powers does not affect the liability of the company in an action for the damage. . . . These provisions, however, only apply where the claim for damage . . . does not exceed £200 [£100 in the 1905 Act], and where written notice of the occurrence of the fire and the intention to claim has been sent to the company within seven days of the occurrence of the damage and particulars of the damage in writing showing the amount

of the claim in money not exceeding £200 have been sent to the company within twenty-one days.

Agricultural land does not include moorland or buildings and agricultural crops do not include those led away or stacked.[41] I have not made a close study of the parliamentary history of this statutory exception, but it appears from debates in the House of Commons in 1922 and 1923 that this exception was probably designed to help the smallholder.[42]

Let us return to Pigou's example of uncompensated damage to surrounding woods caused by sparks from railway engines. This is presumably intended to show how it is possible "for State action to improve on 'natural' tendencies." If we treat Pigou's example as referring to the position before 1905, or as being an arbitrary example (in that he might just as well have written "surrounding buildings" instead of "surrounding woods"), then it is clear that the reason why compensation was not paid must have been that the railway had statutory authority to run steam engines (which relieved it of liability for fires caused by sparks). That this was the legal position was established in 1860, in a case, oddly enough, which concerned the burning of surrounding woods by a railway,[43] and the law on this point has not been changed (apart from the one exception) by a century of railway legislation, including nationalization. If we treat Pigou's example of "uncompensated damage done to surrounding woods by sparks from railway engines" literally, and assume that it refers to the period after 1905, then it is clear that the reason why compensation was not paid must have been that the damage was more than £100 (in the first edition of *The Economics of Welfare*) or more than £200 (in later editions), or that the owner of the wood failed to notify

41. See "Railways and Canals" in *Halsbury's Laws of England*, vol. 31, 474–75, from which this summary of the legal position and all quotations are taken.

42. See 152 Parl. Deb., H.C. 2622–63 (1922); 161 Parl. Deb., H.C. 2935–55 (1923).

43. Vaughan v. Taff Vale Railway Co. 3 H. and N. 743 (Ex. 1858) and 5 H. and N. 679 (Ex. 1860).

the railway in writing within seven days of the fire or did not send particulars of the damage, in writing, within twenty-one days. In the real world, Pigou's example could only exist as a result of a deliberate choice of the legislature. It is not, of course, easy to imagine the construction of a railway in a state of nature. The nearest one can get to this is presumably a railway which uses steam engines "without express statutory authority." However, in this case the railway would be obliged to compensate those whose woods it burnt down. That is to say, compensation would be paid in the absence of governmental action. The only circumstances in which compensation would not be paid would be those in which there had been governmental action. It is strange that Pigou, who clearly thought it desirable that compensation should be paid, should have chosen this particular example to demonstrate how it is possible "for State action to improve on 'natural' tendencies."

Pigou seems to have had a faulty view of the facts of the situation. But it also seems likely that he was mistaken in his economic analysis. It is not necessarily desirable that the railway should be required to compensate those who suffer damage by fires caused by railway engines. I need not show here that, if the railway could make a bargain with everyone having property adjoining the railway line and there were no costs involved in making such bargains, it would not matter whether the railway was liable for damage caused by fires or not. This question has been treated at length in earlier sections. The problem is whether it would be desirable to make the railway liable in conditions in which it is too expensive for such bargains to be made. Pigou clearly thought it was desirable to force the railway to pay compensation, and it is easy to see the kind of argument that would have led him to this conclusion. Suppose a railway is considering whether to run an additional train or to increase the speed of an existing train or to install spark-prevention devices on its engines. If the railway were not liable for fire damage, then, when making these decisions, it would not take into account as a cost the increase in damage resulting from the additional train or the faster train or the failure to install spark-preventing devices. This is the source of the divergence between private and social net products. It results in the railway performing acts which will lower the value of total production—and which it would not do if it were liable for the damage. This can be shown by means of an arithmetical example.

Consider a railway *not* liable for damage by fires caused by sparks from its engines, which runs two trains per day on a certain line. Suppose that running one train per day would enable the railway to perform services worth $150 per annum and running two trains a day would enable the railway to perform services worth $250 per annum. Suppose further that the cost of running one train is $50 per annum and two trains $100 per annum. Under perfect competition, the cost equals the fall in the value of production elsewhere due to the employment of additional factors of production by the railway. Clearly the railway would find it profitable to run two trains per day. But suppose that running one train per day would destroy by fire crops worth (on an average over the year) $60 and two trains a day would result in the destruction of crops worth $120. In these circumstances running one train per day would raise the value of total production, but the running of a second train would reduce the value of total production. The second train would enable additional railway services worth $100 per annum to be performed. But the fall in the value of production elsewhere would be $110 per annum: $50 as a result of the employment of additional factors of production and $60 as a result of the destruction of crops. Since it would be better if the second train were not run and since it would not run if the railway were liable for damage caused to crops, the conclusion that the railway should be made liable for the damage seems irresistible. Undoubtedly it is this kind of reasoning which underlies the Pigovian position.

The conclusion that it would be better if the second train did not run is correct. The conclusion that it is desirable that the railway should be made liable for the damage it causes is wrong. Let us change our assumption concerning the rule of liability. Suppose that the railway is liable for damage from fires caused by sparks from the engine. A farmer on lands adjoining the railway is then in the position that, if his crop is destroyed by fires caused by the railway, he will receive the market price from the railway; but if his crop is not damaged, he will receive the market price by sale. It therefore becomes a matter of indifference to him whether his crop is damaged by fire or not. The position is very different when the railway is not liable. Any crop destruction through railway-caused fires would then reduce the receipts of the farmer. He would therefore take out of cultivation any land for which the damage is likely to be greater than the net return of the land (for reasons explained at length in section III). A change from a regime in which the railway is not liable for damage to one in which it is liable is likely therefore to lead to an increase in the amount of cultivation on lands adjoining the railway. It will also, of course, lead to an increase in the amount of crop destruction due to railway-caused fire.

Let us return to our arithmetical example. Assume that, with the changed rule of liability, there is a doubling in the amount of crop destruction due to railway-caused fire. With one train per day, crops worth $120 would be destroyed each year and two trains per day would lead to the destruction of crops worth $240. We saw previously that it would not be profitable to run the second train if the railway had to pay $60 per annum as compensation for damage. With damage at $120 per annum the loss from running the second train would be $60 greater. But now let us consider the first train. The value of the transport services furnished by the first train is $150. The cost of running the train is $50. The amount that the railway would have to pay out as compensation for damage is $120. It follows that it would not be profitable to run any trains. With the figures in our example we reach the following result: if the railway is not liable for fire damage, two trains per day would be run; if the railway is liable for fire damage, it would cease operations altogether. Does this mean that it is better that there should be no railway? This question can be resolved by considering what would happen to the value of total production if it were decided to exempt the railway from liability for fire damage, thus bringing it into operation (with two trains per day).

The operation of the railway would enable transport services worth $250 to be performed. It would also mean the employment of factors of production which would reduce the value of production elsewhere by $100. Furthermore it would mean the destruction of crops worth $120. The coming of the railway will also have led to the abandonment of cultivation of some land. Since we know that, had this land been cultivated, the value of the crops destroyed by fire would have been $120, and since it is unlikely that the total crop on this land would have been destroyed, it seems reasonable to suppose that the value of the crop yield on this land would have been higher than this. Assume it would have been $160. But the abandonment of cultivation would have released factors of production for employment elsewhere. All we know is that the amount by which the value of production elsewhere will increase will be less than $160. Suppose that it is $150. Then the gain from operating the railway would be $250 (the value of the transport services) minus $100 (the cost of the factors of production) minus $120 (the value of crops destroyed by fire) minus $160 (the fall in the value of crop production due to the abandonment of cultivation) plus $150 (the value of production elsewhere of the released factors of production). Overall, operating the railway will increase the value of total production by $20. With these figures it is clear that it is better that the railway should not be liable for the damage it causes, thus enabling it to operate profitably. Of course, by altering the figures, it could be shown that there are other cases in which it would be desirable that the railway should be liable for the damage it causes. It is enough for my purpose to show that, from an economic point of view, a situation in which there is "uncompensated damage done to surrounding woods by sparks from railway engines" is not necessarily undesirable. Whether it is desirable or not depends on the particular circumstances.

How is it that the Pigovian analysis seems to give the wrong answer? The reason is that Pigou does not seem to have noticed that his analysis is dealing with an entirely different question. The analysis as such is correct. But it is quite illegitimate for Pigou to draw the particular conclusions he does. The question at issue is not whether it is desirable to run an additional train or a faster train or to install smoke-preventing devices; the question at issue is whether it is desirable to have a system in which the railway has to compensate those who suffer damage from the fires which it causes or one in which the railway does not have to compensate them. When an economist is comparing alternative social arrangements, the proper procedure is to compare the total social product yielded by these different arrangements. The comparison of private and social products is neither here nor there. A simple example will demonstrate this. Imagine a town in which there are traffic lights. A motorist approaches an intersection and stops because the light is red. There are no cars approaching the intersection on the other street. If the motorist ignored the red signal, no accident would occur and the total product would increase because the motorist would arrive earlier at his destination. Why does he not do this? The reason is that if he ignored the light he would be fined. The private product from crossing the street is less than the social product. Should we conclude from this that the total product would be greater if there were no fines for failing to obey traffic signals? The Pigovian analysis shows us that it is possible to conceive of better worlds than the one in which we live. But the problem is to devise practical arrangements which will correct defects in one part of the system without causing more serious harm in other parts.

I have examined in considerable detail one example of a divergence between private and social products and I do not propose to make any further examination of Pigou's analytical system. But the main discussion of the problem considered in this article is to be found in that part of chapter 9 in part II which deals with Pigou's second class of divergence, and it is of interest to see how Pigou develops his argument. Pigou's own description of this second class of divergence was quoted at the beginning of this section. Pigou distinguishes between the case in which a person renders services for which he receives no payment and the case in which a person renders disservices and no compensation is given to the injured parties. Our main attention has, of course, centered on this second case. It is therefore rather astonishing to find, as was pointed out to me by Francesco Forte, that the problem of the smoking chimney—the "stock instance"[44] or "classroom example"[45] of the second case—is used by Pigou as an example of the first case (services rendered without payment) and is never mentioned, at any rate explicitly, in connection with the second case.[46] Pigou points out that factory-owners who devote resources to preventing their chimneys from smoking render services for which they receive no payment. The implication, in the light of Pigou's discussion later in the chapter, is that a factory-owner with a smoky chimney should be given a bounty to induce him to install smoke-preventing devices. Most modern economists would suggest that the owner of the factory with the smoky chimney should be taxed. It seems a pity that economists (apart from Forte) do not seem to have noticed this feature of Pigou's treatment, since a realization that the problem could be tackled in either of these two ways would probably have led to an explicit recognition of its reciprocal nature.

In discussing the second case (disservices without compensation to those damaged), Pigou says that they are rendered "when the owner of a site in a residential quarter of a city builds a factory there and so destroys a great part of the amenities of neighbouring sites; or, in a less degree, when he uses his site in such a way as to spoil the lighting of the house opposite; or when he invests resources in erecting buildings in a crowded centre, which by contracting the air-space and the playing room of the neighbourhood, tend to injure the health and efficiency of the families living there."[47] Pigou is, of course, quite right to describe such actions as "uncharged disservices." But he is wrong when he describes these actions as "antisocial."[48] They may or may not be. It is necessary to weigh

44. Dennis Robertson, *Lectures on Economic Principles*, vol. 1 (London: Staples Press, 1957), 162.

45. E. J. Mishan, "The Meaning of Efficiency in Economics," *The Bankers' Magazine* 189 (June 1960): 482.

46. Pigou, *Economics of Welfare*, 184.

47. Ibid., 185–86.

48. Ibid., 186, n. 1. For similar unqualified statements see Pigou's lecture "Some Aspects of the Housing Problems" in B. S. Rowntree and A. C. Pigou, *Lectures on Housing* (Manchester: University Press, 1914).

the harm against the good that will result. Nothing could be more "anti-social" than to oppose any action which causes any harm to anyone.

The example with which Pigou opens his discussion of "uncharged disservices" is not, as I have indicated, the case of the smoky chimney but the case of the overruning rabbits: ". . . incidental uncharged disservices are rendered to third parties when the game-preserving activities of one occupier involve the overrunning of a neighbouring occupier's land by rabbits . . ." This example is of extraordinary interest, not so much because the economic analysis of the case is essentially any different from that of the other examples, but because of the peculiarities of the legal position and the light it throws on the part which economics can play in what is apparently the purely legal question of the delimitation of rights.

The problem of legal liability for the actions of rabbits is part of the general subject of liability for animals.[49] I will, although with reluctance, confine my discussion to rabbits. The early cases relating to rabbits concerned the relations between the lord of the manor and commoners, since, from the thirteenth century on, it became usual for the lord of the manor to stock commons with conies (rabbits), for the sake of both the meat and the fur. But in 1597, in *Boulston*'s case, an action was brought by one landowner against a neighbouring landowner, alleging that the defendant had made coney-burrows and that the conies had increased and had destroyed the plaintiff's corn. The action failed for the reason that

49. See Glanville L. Williams, *Liability for Animals—An Account of the Development and Present Law of Tortious Liability for Animals, Distress Damage Feasant and the Duty to Fence, in Great Britain, Northern Ireland and the Common-law Dominions* (Cambridge, Eng.: Cambridge University Press, 1939). Part Four, "The Action of Nuisance, in Relation to Liability for Animals," 236–62, is especially relevant to our discussion. The problem of liability for rabbits is discussed in this part, 238–47. I do not know how far the common law in the United States regarding liability for animals has diverged from that in Britain. In some western states of the United States, the English common law regarding the duty to fence has not been followed in part because "the considerable amount of open, uncleared land made it a matter of public policy to allow cattle to run at large" (227). This affords a good example of how a different set of circumstances may make it economically desirable to change the legal rule regarding the delimitation of rights.

. . . so soon as the coneys come on his neighbour's land he may kill them, for they are ferae naturae, and he who makes the coney-boroughs has no property in them, and he shall not be punished for the damage which the coneys do in which he has no property, and which the other may lawfully kill.[50]

As *Boulston*'s case has been treated as binding—Bray, J., in 1919, said that he was not aware that *Boulston*'s case has ever been overruled or questioned[51]—Pigou's rabbit example undoubtedly represented the legal position at the time *The Economics of Welfare* was written.[52] And in this case, it is not far from the truth to say that the state of affairs which Pigou describes came about because of an absence of governmental action (at any rate in the form of statutory enactments) and was the result of "natural" tendencies.

Nonetheless, *Boulston*'s case is something of a legal curiosity and Williams makes no secret of his distaste for this decision:

The conception of liability in nuisance as being based upon ownership is the result, apparently, of a confusion with the action of cattle-trespass, and runs counter both to principle and to the medieval authorities on the escape of water, smoke and filth. . . . The prerequisite of any satisfactory treatment of the subject is the final abandonment of the pernicious doctrine in *Boulston*'s case. . . . Once *Boulston*'s case disappears, the way will be clear for a rational restatement of the whole subject, on lines that will harmonize with the principles prevailing in the rest of the law of nuisance.[53]

The judges in *Boulston*'s case were, of course, aware that their view of the matter depended on distinguishing this case from one involving nuisance:

50. Coke (vol. 3) 104 b. 77 Eng. Rep., 216, 217.
51. See Stearn v. Prentice Bros. Ltd. [1919] 1 K.B., 395, 397.
52. I have not looked into recent cases. The legal position has also been modified by statutory enactments.
53. Williams, *Liability for Animals*, 242, 258.

This cause is not like to the cases put, on the other side, of erecting a lime-kiln, dye-house, or the like; for there the annoyance is by the act of the parties who make them; but it is not so here, for the conies of themselves went into the plaintiff's land, and he might take them when they came upon his land, and make profit of them.[54]

Williams comments:

Once more the atavistic idea is emerging that the animals are guilty and not the landowner. It is not, of course, a satisfactory principle to introduce into a modern law of nuisance. If A. erects a house or plants a tree so that the rain runs or drips from it on to B.'s land, this is A.'s act for which he is liable; but if A. introduces rabbits into his land so that they escape from it into B.'s this is the act of the rabbits for which A. is not liable—such is the specious distinction resulting from *Boulston*'s case.[55]

It has to be admitted that the decision in *Boulston*'s case seems a little odd. A man may be liable for damage caused by smoke or unpleasant smells, without it being necessary to determine whether he owns the smoke or the smell. And the rule in *Boulston*'s case has not always been followed in cases dealing with other animals. For example, in *Bland v. Yates*,[56] it was decided that an injunction could be granted to prevent someone from keeping an *unusual and excessive* collection of manure in which flies bred and subsequently infested a neighbour's house. The question of who owned the flies was not raised. An economist would not wish to object because legal reasoning sometimes appears a little odd. But there is a sound economic reason for supporting Williams' view that the problem of liability for animals (and particularly rabbits) should be brought within the ordinary law of nuisance. The reason is not that a

---

54. Boulston v. Hardy, Cro Eliz., 547, 548, 77 Eng. Rep. 216.
55. Williams, *Liability for Animals*, 243.
56. Bland v. Yates, 58 Sol. J. 612 (1913–1914).

man who harbours rabbits is solely responsible for the damage; the man whose crops are eaten is equally responsible. And given that the costs of market transactions make a rearrangement of rights impossible unless we know the particular circumstances, we cannot say whether it is desirable or not to make the man who harbours rabbits responsible for the damage committed by the rabbits on neighbouring properties. The objection to the rule in *Boulston*'s case is that, under it, the harbourer of rabbits can *never* be liable. It fixes the rule of liability at one pole: and this is as undesirable, from an economic point of view, as fixing the rule at the other pole and making the harbourer of rabbits always liable. But, as we saw in section VII, the law of nuisance, as it is in fact handled by the courts, is flexible and allows for a comparison of the utility of an act with the harm it produces. As Williams says: "The whole law of nuisance is an attempt to reconcile and compromise between conflicting interests. . . ."[57] To bring the problem of rabbits within the ordinary law of nuisance would not mean *inevitably* making the harbourer of rabbits liable for damage committed by the rabbits. This is not to say that the sole task of the courts in such cases is to make a comparison between the harm and the utility of an act. Nor is it to be expected that the courts will always decide correctly after making such a comparison. But unless the courts act very foolishly, the ordinary law of nuisance would seem likely to give economically more satisfactory results than adopting a rigid rule. Pigou's case of the overrunning rabbits affords an excellent example of how problems of law and economics are interrelated, even though the correct policy to follow would seem to be different from that envisioned by Pigou.

Pigou allows one exception to his conclusion that there is a divergence between private and social products in the rabbit example. He adds: ". . . unless . . . the two occupiers stand in the relation of landlord and tenant, so that compensation is given in an adjustment of the rent."[58] This qualification is rather surprising, since Pigou's first class of divergence is largely

57. Williams, *Liability for Animals,* 259.
58. Pigou, *Economics of Welfare,* 185.

concerned with the difficulties of drawing up satisfactory contracts between landlords and tenants. In fact, all the recent cases on the problem of rabbits cited by Williams involved disputes between landlords and tenants concerning sporting rights.[59] Pigou seems to make a distinction between the case in which no contract is possible (the second class) and that in which the contract is unsatisfactory (the first class). Thus he says that the second class of divergence between private and social net product

> cannot, like divergences due to tenancy laws, be mitigated by a modification of the contractual relation between any two contracting parties, because the divergence arises out of a service or disservice rendered to persons other than the contracting parties.[60]

But the reason why some activities are not the subject of contracts is exactly the same as the reason why some contracts are commonly unsatisfactory—it would cost too much to put the matter right. Indeed, the two cases are really the same, since the contracts are unsatisfactory because they do not cover certain activities. The exact bearing of the discussion of the first class of divergence on Pigou's main argument is difficult to discover. He shows that in some circumstances contractual relations between landlord and tenant may result in a divergence between private and social products.[61] But he also goes on to show that government-enforced compensation schemes and rent controls will also produce divergences.[62] Furthermore, he shows that, when the government is in a similar position to a private landlord, for example, when granting a franchise to a public utility, exactly the same difficulties arise as when private individuals are involved.[63] The discussion is interesting, but I have been unable to discover what general

59. Williams, *Liability for Animals,* 244–47.
60. Pigou, *Economics of Welfare,* 192.
61. Ibid., 174–75.
62. Ibid., 177–83.
63. Ibid., 175–77.

conclusions about economic policy, if any, Pigou expects us to draw from it.

Indeed, Pigou's treatment of the problems considered in this article is extremely elusive, and the discussion of his views raises almost insuperable difficulties of interpretation. Consequently it is impossible to be sure that one has understood what Pigou really meant. Nevertheless, it is difficult to resist the conclusion, extraordinary though this may be in an economist of Pigou's stature, that the main source of this obscurity is that Pigou had not thought his position through.

IX. The Pigovian Tradition

It is strange that a doctrine as faulty as that developed by Pigou should have been so influential, although part of its success has probably been due to the lack of clarity in the exposition. Not being clear, it was never clearly wrong. Curiously enough, this obscurity in the source has not prevented the emergence of a fairly well defined oral tradition. What economists think they learn from Pigou, and what they tell their students, which I term the Pigovian tradition, is reasonably clear. I propose to show the inadequacy of this Pigovian tradition by demonstrating that both the analysis and the policy conclusions which it supports are incorrect.

I do not propose to justify my view as to the prevailing opinion by copious references to the literature. I do this partly because the treatment in the literature is usually so fragmentary, often involving little more than a reference to Pigou plus some explanatory comment, that detailed examination would be inappropriate. But the main reason for this lack of reference is that the doctrine, although based on Pigou, must have been largely the product of an oral tradition. Certainly economists with whom I have discussed these problems have shown a unanimity of opinion which is quite remarkable considering the meagre treatment accorded this subject in the literature. No doubt there are some economists who do not share the usual view, but they must represent a small minority of the profession.

The approach to the problems under discussion is through an examination of the value of physical production. The private product is the value of the additional product resulting from a particular activity of a business. The social product equals the private product minus the fall in the value of production elsewhere for which no compensation is paid by the business. Thus, if 10 units of a factor (and no other factors) are used by a business to make a certain product with a value of $105; and the owner of this factor is not compensated for their use, which he is unable to prevent; and these 10 units of the factor would yield products in their best alternative use worth $100; then, the social product is $105 minus $100 or $5. If the business now pays for one unit of the factor and its price equals the value of its marginal product, then the social product rises to $15. If two units are paid for, the social product rises to $25 and so on until it reaches $105 when all units of the factor are paid for. It is not difficult to see why economists have so readily accepted this rather odd procedure. The analysis focuses on the individual business decision, and since the use of certain resources are not allowed for in costs, receipts are reduced by the same amount. But, of course, this means that the value of the social product has no social significance whatsoever. It seems to me preferable to use the opportunity-cost concept and to approach these problems by comparing the value of the product yielded by factors in alternative uses or by alternative arrangements. The main advantage of a pricing system is that it leads to the employment of factors in places where the value of the product yielded is greatest and does so at less cost than alternative systems (I leave aside that a pricing system also eases the problem of the redistribution of income). But if, through some God-given natural harmony, factors flowed to the places where the value of the product yielded was greatest without any use of the pricing system and consequently there was no compensation, I would find it a source of surprise rather than a cause for dismay.

The definition of the social product is queer but this does not mean that the conclusions for policy drawn from the analysis are necessarily wrong. However, there are bound to be dangers in an approach which diverts attention from the basic issues, and there can be little doubt that it has been responsible for some of the errors in current doctrine. The belief that it is desirable that the business which causes harmful effects should be forced to compensate those who suffer damage (which was exhaustively discussed in section VIII in connection with Pigou's railway-sparks example) is undoubtedly the result of not comparing the total product obtainable with alternative social arrangements.

The same fault is to be found in proposals for solving the problem of harmful effects by the use of taxes or bounties. Pigou lays considerable stress on this solution, although he is, as usual, lacking in detail and qualified in his support.[64] Modern economists tend to think exclusively in terms of taxes and in a very precise way. The tax should be equal to the damage done and should therefore vary with the amount of the harmful effect. As it is not proposed that the proceeds of the tax should be paid to those suffering the damage, this solution is not the same as that which would force a business to pay compensation to those damaged by its actions, although economists generally do not seem to have noticed this and tend to treat the two solutions as being identical.

Assume that a factory which emits smoke is set up in a district previously free from smoke pollution, causing damage valued at $100 per annum. Assume that the taxation solution is adopted and that the factory-owner is taxed $100 per annum as long as the factory emits the smoke. Assume further that a smoke-preventing device costing $90 per annum to run is available. In these circumstances, the smoke-preventing device would be installed. Damage of $100 would have been avoided at an expenditure of $90 and the factory-owner would be better off by $10 per annum. Yet the position achieved may not be optimal. Suppose that those who suffer the damage could avoid it by moving to other locations or by taking various precautions which would cost them, or be equivalent to a loss in income of, $40 per annum. Then there would be a gain in the value of production of $50 if the factory continued to emit its smoke and those now in the district moved elsewhere or made other adjustments to avoid the damage. If the factory-owner is to be

64. Ibid., 192–94, 381, and A. C. Pigou, *A Study in Public Finance*, 3rd ed. (London: Macmillan & Co., 1947), 94–100.

made to pay a tax equal to the damage caused, it would clearly be desirable to institute a double tax system and to make residents of the district pay an amount equal to the additional cost incurred by the factory-owner (or the consumers of his products) in order to avoid the damage. In these conditions, people would not stay in the district or would take other measures to prevent the damage from occurring, when the costs of doing so were less than the costs that would be incurred by the producer to reduce the damage (the producer's object, of course, being not so much to reduce the damage as to reduce the tax payments). A tax system which was confined to a tax on the producer for damage caused would tend to lead to unduly high costs being incurred for the prevention of damage. Of course, this could be avoided if it were possible to base the tax, not on the damage caused, but on the fall in the value of production (in its widest sense) resulting from the emission of smoke. But to do so would require a detailed knowledge of individual preferences, and I am unable to imagine how the data needed for such a taxation system could be assembled. Indeed, the proposal to solve the smoke-pollution and similar problems by the use of taxes bristles with difficulties: the problem of calculation, the difference between average and marginal damage, the interrelations of the damage suffered on different properties, etc. But it is unnecessary to examine these problems here. It is enough for my purpose to show that, even if the tax is exactly adjusted to equal the damage that would be done to neighbouring properties as a result of the emissions of each additional puff of smoke, the tax would not necessarily bring about optimal conditions. An increase in the number of people living or of businesses operating in the vicinity of the smoke-emitting factory will increase the amount of harm produced by a given emission of smoke. The tax that would be imposed would therefore increase with an increase in the number of those in the vicinity. This will tend to lead to a decrease in the value of production of the factors employed by the factory, either because a reduction in production due to the tax will result in factors being used elsewhere in ways which are less valuable, or because factors will be diverted to produce means for reducing the amount of smoke emitted. But people deciding to establish themselves in the vicinity of the factory will not take into account this fall in the value of production which results from their presence. This failure to take into account costs imposed on others is comparable to the action of a factory-owner in not taking into account the harm resulting from his emission of smoke. Without the tax, there may be too much smoke and too few people in the vicinity of the factory; but with the tax there may be too little smoke and too many people in the vicinity of the factory. There is no reason to suppose that either of these results is necessarily preferable.

I need not devote much space to discussing the similar error involved in the suggestion that smoke-producing factories should, by means of zoning regulations, be removed from the districts in which the smoke causes harmful effects. When the change in the location of the factory results in a reduction in production, this obviously needs to be taken into account and weighed against the harm which would result from the factory remaining in that location. The aim of such regulations should not be to eliminate smoke pollution but rather to secure the optimum amount of smoke pollution, this being the amount which will maximize the value of production.

X. A Change of Approach

It is my belief that the failure of economists to reach correct conclusions about the treatment of harmful effects cannot be ascribed simply to a few slips in analysis. It stems from basic defects in the current approach to problems of welfare economics. What is needed is a change of approach. Analysis in terms of divergences between private and social products concentrates attention on particular deficiencies in the system and tends to nourish the belief that any measure which will remove the deficiency is necessarily desirable. It diverts attention from those other changes in the system which are inevitably associated with the corrective measure, changes which may well produce more harm than the original deficiency. In the preceding sections of this article, we have seen many examples of this. But it is not necessary to approach the problem in this way. Economists who study problems of the firm habitually use an opportunity-cost approach and compare the receipts obtained from a given combination of factors with alternative business arrangements. It would seem desirable to use a similar approach when dealing with questions of economic policy and to compare the total product yielded by alternative social arrangements. In this article, the analysis has been confined, as is usual in this part of economics, to comparisons of the value of production, as measured by the market. But it is, of course, desirable that the choice among different social arrangements for the solution of economic problems should be carried out in broader terms than this and that the total effect of these arrangements in all spheres of life should be taken into account. As Frank H. Knight has so often emphasized, problems of welfare economics must ultimately dissolve into a study of aesthetics and morals.

A second feature of the usual treatment of the problems discussed in this article is that the analysis proceeds in terms of a comparison between a state of laissez faire and some kind of ideal world. This approach inevitably leads to a looseness of thought since the nature of the alternatives being compared is never clear. In a state of laissez faire, is there a monetary, a legal, or a political system, and if so, what are they? In an ideal world, would there be a monetary, a legal, or a political system, and if so, what would they be? The answers to all these questions are shrouded in mystery and every man is free to draw whatever conclusions he likes. Actually, very little analysis is required to show that an ideal world is better than a state of laissez faire, unless the definitions of a state of laissez faire and an ideal world happen to be the same. But the whole discussion is largely irrelevant for questions of economic policy since, whatever we may have in mind as our ideal world, it is clear that we have not yet discovered how to get to it from where we are. A better approach would seem to be to start our analysis with a situation approximating that which actually exists, to examine the effects of a proposed policy change, and to attempt to decide whether the new situation would be, in total, better or worse than the original one. In this way, conclusions for policy would have some relevance to the actual situation.

A final reason for the failure to develop a theory adequate to handle the problem of harmful effects stems from a faulty concept of a factor of production. This is usually thought of as a physical entity which the businessman acquires and uses (an acre of land, a ton of fertilizer) instead of as a right to perform certain (physical) actions. We may speak of a person owning land and using it as a factor of production, but what the land-owner in fact possesses is the right to carry out a circumscribed list of actions. The rights of a land-owner are not unlimited. It is not even always possible for him to remove the land to another place, for instance, by quarrying it. And although it may be possible for him to exclude some people from using "his" land, this may not be true of others. For example, some people may have the right to cross the land. Furthermore, it may or may not be possible to erect certain types of building or to grow certain crops or to use particular drainage systems on the land. This does not come about simply because of governmental regulation. It would be equally true under the common law. In fact, it would be true under any system of law. A system in which the rights of individuals were unlimited would be one in which there were no rights to acquire.

If factors of production are thought of as rights, it becomes easier to understand that the right to do something which has a harmful effect (such as the creation of smoke, noise, smells, etc.) is also a factor of production. Just as we may use a piece of land in such a way as to prevent someone else from crossing it, or parking his car, or building his house upon it, so we may use it in such a way as to deny him a view or quiet or unpolluted air. The cost of exercising a right (of using a factor of production) is always the loss which is suffered elsewhere in consequence of the exercise of that right—the inability to cross land, to park a car, to build a house, to enjoy a view, to have peace and quiet, or to breathe clean air.

It would clearly be desirable if the only actions performed were those in which what was gained was worth more than what was lost. But in choosing among social arrangements within the context of which individual decisions are made, we have to bear in mind that a change in the existing system which will lead to an improvement in some decisions may well lead

SIX

Notes on the Problem of Social Cost

I. The Coase Theorem

I did not originate the phrase, the "Coase Theorem," nor its precise formulation, both of which we owe to Stigler. However, it is true that his statement of the theorem is based on work of mine in which the same thought is found, although expressed rather differently. I first advanced the proposition which has been transformed into the Coase Theorem in an article on "The Federal Communications Commission." I there said: "Whether a newly discovered cave belongs to the man who discovered it, the man on whose land the entrance to the cave is located, or the man who owns the surface under which the cave is situated is no doubt dependent on the law of property. But the law merely determines the person with whom it is necessary to make a contract to obtain the use of a cave. Whether the cave is used for storing bank records, as a natural gas reservoir, or for growing mushrooms depends, not on the law of property, but on whether the bank, the natural gas corporation, or the mushroom concern will pay the most in order to be able to use the cave."[1] I then indicated that this proposition, which seems difficult to dispute when it relates to the right to use a cave, could also be applied to the right to emit electrical radiations (or to generate smoke pollution), and I illustrated my argument by considering the case of *Sturges v. Bridgman,* which involved a doctor disturbed by noise and vibration resulting from the operation of a confectioner's machinery. Using a line of argument which must now be quite familiar, I showed that,

1. R. H. Coase, "The Federal Communications Commission," *The Journal of Law and Economics* (October 1959): 25.

whether or not the confectioner had the right to make the noise or vibration, that right would in fact be acquired by the party to whom it was most valuable (just as would be the case with the newly discovered cave). I summed up by saying that while "the delimitation of rights is an essential prelude to market transactions . . . the ultimate result (which maximizes the value of production) is independent of the legal decision."[2] This is the essence of the Coase Theorem. I repeated the argument at greater length in "The Problem of Social Cost," making clear that this result was dependent on the assumption of zero transaction costs.

Stigler states the Coase Theorem in the following words: ". . . under perfect competition private and social costs will be equal."[3] Since, with zero transaction costs, as Stigler also points out, monopolies would be induced to "act like competitors,"[4] it is perhaps enough to say that, with zero transaction costs, private and social costs will be equal. It will be observed that Stigler's statement of the Coase Theorem differs from the way I expressed the same thought in my article. There I spoke of the value of production being maximized. There is, however, no inconsistency. Social cost represents the greatest value that factors of production would yield in an alternative use. Producers, however, who are normally only interested in maximizing their own incomes, are not concerned with social cost and will only undertake an activity if the value of the product of the factors employed is greater than their private cost (the amount these factors would *earn* in their best alternative employment). But if private cost is equal to social cost, it follows that producers will only engage in an activity if the value of the product of the factors employed is greater than the value which they would yield in their best alternative use. That is to say, with zero transaction costs, the value of production would be maximized.

2. Ibid., 27.
3. George J. Stigler, *The Theory of Price,* 3rd ed. (New York: Macmillan Co., 1966), 113.
4. George J. Stigler, "The Law and Economics of Public Policy: A Plea to the Scholars," *Journal of Legal Studies* 1, no. 1 (1972): 12.

The discussion of the Coase Theorem in the economics literature has been very extensive and I cannot hope to deal with all the points that have been raised. Some of the criticisms, however, strike at the heart of my argument and have been so persistently made, often by extremely able economists, that it is meet that I should deal with them, particularly since these criticisms are, in my view, for the most part, either invalid, unimportant or irrelevant. Even those sympathetic to my point of view have often misunderstood my argument, a result which I ascribe to the extraordinary hold which Pigou's approach has had on the minds of modern economists. I can only hope that these notes will help to weaken that hold. Whether I am right or not, they will at least serve to make clear the character of my argument.

II. Will Wealth Be Maximized?

A fundamental point is whether it is reasonable to assume, as I did, that, when there are zero transaction costs, negotiations will lead to an agreement which maximizes wealth. It has been argued that this is an erroneous assumption, an objection which has added weight because it has been advanced by, among others, Samuelson. He makes but two references to "The Problem of Social Cost," both in footnotes, but his point is essentially the same on both occasions. In the first he says: "Unconstrained self-interest will in such cases [negotiations over smoke nuisances and the like] lead to the insoluble bilateral monopoly problem with all its indeterminacies and nonoptimalities."[5] And in the second he says: ". . . a problem of pricing two or more inputs that can be used in common is not solved by reducing it to a determinate maximized total whose allocation among the parts is an indeterminate problem in multilateral monopoly."[6]

5. Paul A. Samuelson, "Modern Economics Realities and Individualism," *The Texas Quarterly* (Summer 1963): 128; reprinted in *The Collected Scientific Papers of Paul A. Samuelson*, vol. 2 (Cambridge, Mass.: MIT Press, 1966), 1411.
6. Paul A. Samuelson, "The Monopolistic Competition Revolution," in *Monopolistic Competition Theory: Studies in Impact; Essays in Honor of Edward H. Chamberlin* ed. Robert E. Kuenne (New York: Wiley, 1967), 105; reprinted in *The Collected Scientific Papers of Paul A. Samuelson*, 3: 36.

Samuelson's comments embody a view which he has long held and which was originally used to criticize the analysis of a more formidable adversary. Edgeworth had argued in *Mathematical Psychics* (1881) that two individuals engaged in exchanging goods would end on the "contract curve" because, if they did not, there would remain positions to which they could move by exchange which would make both of them better off. Edgeworth implicitly assumed that there was costless "contracting" and "recontracting"; and I have often thought that a subconscious memory of the argument in *Mathematical Psychics,* which I studied more than fifty years ago, may have played a part in leading me to formulate the proposition which has come to be termed the "Coase Theorem." Samuelson says this of Edgeworth's argument in his *Foundations of Economic Analysis*: ". . . from any point off the contract curve there exists a movement toward it which would be beneficial to both individuals. This is not the same thing as to say, with Edgeworth, that exchange will in fact necessarily cease somewhere on the contract curve; for in many types of bilateral monopoly a final equilibrium may be reached off the contract curve."[7] Later Samuelson adds this: ". . . our experience with man as a social animal suggest[s] that one [cannot] safely predict, as a factual matter, that 'educated and intelligent men of good will' in point of fact tend to move to the generalized contract locus. As an empirical statement of fact we cannot agree with the assertion of Edgeworth that bilateral monopolists must end up somewhere on the contract curve. They may end up elsewhere, because one or both is unwilling to discuss the possibility of making a mutually favorable movement for fear that the discussion may imperil the existing tolerable *status quo*."[8] Samuelson's explanation in the *Foundations* of why two individuals may fail to end up on the contract curve is that they may be unwilling to initiate negotiations leading to an exchange which could make both of them better off, because to do so may have as its result an agreement which leaves one or both

7. Paul A. Samuelson, *Foundations of Economic Analysis* (Cambridge, Mass.: Harvard University Press, 1947), 238.

8. Ibid., 251.

of them worse off than they were before. This contention is not easy to understand. If there already existed a contract between the parties, so that mutual agreement was required for its modification, there would seem to be no obstacle hindering the opening of negotiations. And if there were no contract, there is no *status quo* to imperil. For exchange to take place, there has to be an agreement about the terms of the exchange, and given that this is so, I would not expect the parties to choose terms which make both of them worse off than they need be. Perhaps what Samuelson had in mind was that there may be no contract and no exchange because the parties cannot agree on the terms, given that this affects their respective gains from the exchange. This seems to have been Samuelson's position in 1967. He then said that "the rational self-interest of each of two free wills does not necessitate that there will emerge, even in the most idealized game-theoretic situation, a Pareto-optimal solution that maximizes the sum of two opponent's profits, *in advance of and without regard to how that maximized profit is to be divided up among them.* Except by fiat of the economic analyst or by his tautologically redefining what constitutes 'nonrational' behavior we cannot rule out a non-Pareto-optimal outcome" (italics in original).[9]

It is certainly true that we cannot rule out such an outcome if the parties are unable to agree on the terms of exchange, and it is therefore impossible to argue that two individuals negotiating an exchange *must* end up on the contract curve, even in a world of zero transaction costs in which the parties have, in effect, an eternity in which to bargain. However, there is good reason to suppose that the proportion of cases in which no agreement is reached will be small.

As Samuelson himself points out, situations in which the price at which a supplier is willing to sell is less than the price at which a demander is willing to buy, and in which the parties therefore have to reach an agreement on the price, are "ubiquitous in real life."[10] Samuelson gives an example: "If my

9. See Samuelson, *Collected Scientific Papers*, 3:35.
10. Ibid., 36.

secretary has been trained to my ways and I have been trained to hers, there is a range of indeterminacy to the imputation of our joint product. Without her I can find some kind of substitute but not necessarily, per dollar of cost, a close substitute. On the other hand, were I to turn tomorrow to a career in plumbing, her considerable investment in mastering the vocabulary of my peculiar kind of economics might become totally valueless. If I were poised on the margin of indifference it might pay her to make me side payments to tempt me to eschew a career with the monkey wrench."[11]

This is a fanciful example of a very common situation, whether we are considering purchases of raw materials, machinery, land, buildings, or labour services. Of course, the competition of substitutes normally very much narrows the range within which the agreed price must fall, but it must be very rare indeed for both the buyer and the seller to be indifferent as to whether a transaction goes through. And yet we observe that raw materials, machinery, land, and buildings are bought and sold and even professors manage to have secretaries. We do not usually seem to let the problem of the division of the gain stand in the way of making an agreement. Nor is this surprising. Those who find it impossible to conclude agreements will find that they neither buy nor sell and consequently will usually have no income. Traits which lead to such an outcome have little survival value, and we may assume (certainly I do) that normally human beings do not possess them and are willing to "split the difference." Samuelson asserts as "an empirical statement of fact" that people, in the situation analyzed by Edgeworth, will not necessarily end up somewhere on the contract curve. This is no doubt correct, but a fact of even more significance is that normally we would expect them to end up there. Samuelson, discussing the hypothetical example in which he is considering taking up plumbing, points out that "it might pay" his secretary "to make me side payments to tempt me to eschew a career with the monkey wrench."

11. Ibid.

It is certainly true that his secretary might not agree to make these side payments, or, what comes to the same thing, to accept a reduction in salary even though this would make her (and Samuelson) better off; or Samuelson might worsen his situation (and hers) by taking up plumbing because in his view she was not willing to reduce her salary enough; but I would regard such outcomes as being, in these circumstances, most unlikely, particularly in a regime of zero transaction costs.

Samuelson also lays stress on the indeterminacy of the final result. While this is true for purchases of all kinds and therefore applies to all of economic analysis, the existence of indeterminacy, as Edgeworth showed, does not of itself imply that the result is non-optimal. Furthermore, that the respective gains of the two parties are indeterminate is irrelevant to the problem I was discussing in "The Problem of Social Cost," the assignment to individuals and firms of rights to perform certain actions and its effect on what is produced and sold. In any case, there is no reason to suppose that the degree of indeterminacy over the sharing of the gains would be greater in negotiations over the rights to emit smoke than in transactions which economists are more accustomed to handle, such as the purchase of a house.

III. The Coase Theorem and Rents

Most objections to the Coase Theorem seem to underestimate what costless transacting could accomplish. But some criticisms raise questions of a more general character. For example, it is said that the Coase Theorem fails to take into account the crucial role played by the existence or non-existence of rents. The term "rent" in this context is used to denote the difference between what a factor of production earns in the activity under discussion and what it could otherwise earn. I had analyzed the problem by considering what happened to the net return to the land. But there is no difficulty in rephrasing the argument in terms of rent. It does little more than restate in other words my original argument, but some economists may find this approach more congenial.

The relation of the existence of rents to my analysis was first discussed by Wellisz.[12] This way of looking at things has since been used as the basis for arguing that my conclusion is wrong by Regan[13] and Auten, among others. The point is stated succinctly by Auten: "In Coase's examples the results will . . . vary with liability depending on the Ricardian rents of polluters and receptors. If both polluter and receptor operate on marginal land the polluter must cease operations in the long run if liable, and the receptor will be driven out if liable."[14] The contention is plausible. The land is marginal and earns no return, while the other factors employed are in perfectly elastic supply and do not earn more in this use than in some alternative use. In these circumstances it would seem obvious that, if those responsible for the pollution have to pay compensation for the damage caused, the factors of production (other than land) used in the activity which pollutes will leave this employment, since any payment for the damage caused would reduce their earnings below what they would be elsewhere. But suppose that those polluting are not liable. Those who suffer the damage resulting from the pollution will find that, taking the damage into account, they now earn less than they would in an alternative employment and will therefore be better off by moving elsewhere. All this would seem to suggest, contrary to what I had said, that the legal position does affect the outcome. Auten's argument, though plausible, is, I believe, wrong. Since in these conditions no one's income could be increased by possession of the right to pollute, no one would pay anything for it. The price would therefore be zero. How can one say that someone does not have the right to pollute when for a zero price he can acquire it? How can one say that someone must suffer damage when for a zero price he can avoid it? Liability and nonliability are interchangeable at will. Polluters and re-

12. Stanislaw Wellisz, "On External Diseconomics and the Government-assisted Invisible Hand," *Economica*, n.s., 31 (November 1964): 345–62.

13. Donald H. Regan, "The Problem of Social Cost Revisited," *Journal of Law and Economics* 15, no. 2 (October 1972): 427–37.

14. Gerald E. Auten, "Discussion," in *Theory and Measurement of Economic Externalities*, ed. Steven A. Y. Lin (New York: Academic Press, 1976), 38.

ceptors, to use Auten's terms, are equally likely to stay or leave. What will happen is completely unaffected by the initial legal position.

Rent consists of the difference between what a factor of production earns in a given activity and what it could earn in the best alternative activity. The factors engaged in an activity would be willing, if need be, to pay an amount of money up to slightly less than the sum of their rents to allow their employment in that activity to continue, because, even after taking this payment into account, they would be better off than if they had to move to their best alternative. Similarly, they would be willing to abandon an activity in return for any payment greater than the sum of their rents, since, including this payment, they would be better off by moving to their best alternative than by continuing in this activity. Given that this is so, it becomes easy to show that, with zero transaction costs, the allocation of resources will remain the same whatever the legal position regarding liability for damage. To simplify the discussion, I will call the sum of the rents of the factors engaged in an activity the "rents" and will examine the same example as in my original article, that of cattle which roam and destroy crops. I will call the factors of production which are engaged in raising cattle the "ranchers" and the factors of production which are engaged in cultivating crops the "farmers."

Since the rents represent the increase in the value of production (and therefore of incomes) from undertaking a particular activity rather than the best alternative, it follows that the value of production, as measured on the market, is maximized when rents are maximized. If the farmers cultivated their crops (and there were no ranchers), the increase in the value of production resulting from their operations would be measured by the rents of the factors engaged in farming. If the ranchers raised their cattle, (and there were no farmers) the increase in the value of production resulting from their operations would be measured by the rents of the factors engaged in ranching. If there were both ranchers and farmers but no damage to crops as a result of the roaming of the cattle, the increase in the value of production would be measured by the sum of the rents of the farmers and ranchers. However, suppose that, given ranching, some crops would be destroyed by the roaming of the cattle. In this case, when farming and ranching are carried on simultaneously, the increase in the value of production is measured by the sum of the rents of both the farmers and the ranchers (as defined) minus the value of the crops destroyed by the cattle.

Suppose first that the damage to the crops with simultaneous ranching and farming is valued at less than either the rents of the ranchers or the rents of the farmers. If the ranchers were liable for the damage inflicted by their cattle, they could compensate the farmers and continue their operations and still be better off than if they abandoned ranching by an amount equal to their rents minus the value of the damage. If the ranchers were not liable, the maximum the farmers would pay to induce the ranchers to stop their operations would be the value of the destroyed crops. This is less than the additional sum the ranchers could earn by continuing to operate rather than moving to their best alternative employment. The farmers would therefore be unable to induce the ranchers to stop their operations. As the rents of the farmers are greater than the value of the destroyed crops, the farmers would still enjoy a net gain from continuing to farm. Whatever the legal position, both ranchers and farmers would continue to operate. It is easy to show that this will maximize the value of production. If the farmers' rents are $100 and the ranchers' rents are also $100 and the value of the crops destroyed is $50, the value of production will be greater than it would otherwise be if both farmers and ranchers continue to operate. In these conditions the increase in the value of production would be $150 (the sum of the rents minus the value of the crops destroyed). If either the farmers or the ranchers discontinued operations, the increase in the value of productions would fall to $100.

Now consider what would happen if the damage to the crops were valued at less than the rents of the ranchers but more than the rents of the farmers. Assume first that the ranchers are liable for the damage brought about by their cattle. If the ranchers compensated the farmers for their crop loss (which they could do since their rents are greater than the value of the crop damage), the farmers would earn the same amount as if the damage had not occurred (payment by the ranchers for the crops destroyed would be substituted for sale on the market). But the rents of the farmers are less than the value of the crops destroyed. The farmers would agree not to cultivate for any payment which is greater than their rents. The ranchers would be better off if they induced the farmers not to grow their crops (and thus bring to an end crop destruction) by making a payment which is less than the value of crop damage. In the assumed circumstances a bargain would be struck by which, for a payment by the ranchers greater than the farmers' rents but less than the value of the crop damage, the farmers would not engage in cultivation. Now assume that the ranchers are not liable for crop damage. As the damage that the farmers would suffer would be greater than their rents, the farmers would earn less than in their best alternative activity if they cultivated their crops and they would therefore not engage in cultivation unless they could induce the ranchers to give up their operations. But the maximum amount which the farmers would pay to bring this about would be slightly less than their rents. As the ranchers' rents from continuing their activities (with its attendant crop destruction) are greater than the farmers' rents, the farmers would be unable to make a payment sufficiently great to induce the ranchers to cease their operations. In these circumstances, just as was true when the ranchers were liable for crop damage, crop cultivation would not take place, the farmers would engage in their best alternative occupation, while the ranchers would continue to operate. As before, a change in the legal position is without effect on the allocation of resources. Furthermore, the resulting allocation is the one which maximizes the value of production. Assume that the rents of the ranchers are $100, the value of the crop damage $50, and the rents of the farmers $25. If the ranchers and farmers both continued their operations, the increase in the value of production would be $75 ($100 plus $25 minus $50). If the ranchers discontinued their operations, the increase in the value of production would be $25 (the rents of the farmers), while if the ranchers alone continued to operate, the increase in the value of production would be $100 (the rents of the ranchers).

Let us now reverse the situation which we have just discussed and consider what would happen if the value of the crop damage is greater than the rents of the ranchers but less than the rents of the farmers. Assume first that the ranchers are liable for the damage. Since the amount the ranchers would have to pay to compensate the farmers would be more than their rents, ranching would not take place and the farmers would continue their cultivation. Now assume that the ranchers are not liable. If the ranchers continued to operate, the farmers would be willing, if they had to, to endure the crop damage since this is less than their rents. But there is a preferable alternative open to them. The rents of the ranchers are less than the value of the damage which their cattle inflict on the farmers' crops. The ranchers would be willing to cease operations in return for any payment greater than their rents. The farmers would be willing to make such a payment, providing that it was less than the value of the crop damage. But this is what the conditions are assumed to be. It follows that a bargain would be made by which the ranchers would not undertake their operations. As before, the outcome remains the same whatever the legal position. And once again, the value of production is maximized. Assume that the rents of the ranchers are $25, the value of crop damage $50, and the rents of the farmers $100. If the ranchers and farmers both continued their operations, the increase in the value of production would be $75 ($25 plus $100 minus $50). If the ranchers alone continued their operations, the increase in the value of production would be $25 (the rents of the ranchers) while if the farmers alone continued to operate, the increase would be $100 (the rents of the farmers).

Let us now consider the case in which the value of the damage to the crops is greater than the rents of either the ranchers or the farmers. Assume first that the rents of the ranchers are greater than the rents of the farmers. If the ranchers were liable for the crop damage caused by their cattle and had to compensate the farmers, it is clear that the ranchers would have to abandon their operations. But this is not the only course open to them. The farmers would be happy not to grow their crops for a payment greater than their rents. In these circumstances the ranchers would be willing to pay the farmers an amount greater than the farmers' rents (but less than their own rents) to induce the farmers not to cultivate, which would bring to an end crop destruction, eliminate the need for compensation from the ranchers, and leave the ranchers better off. If the ranchers were not liable for damage, the value of crop damage would exceed the rents of the farmers, who would not therefore engage in crop cultivation but would choose their best alternative, unless they could induce the ranchers to stop their operations. The maximum the farmers could offer to accomplish this and still be better off would be slightly less than their own rents. But as the rents of the ranchers are greater than the rents of the farmers, the ranchers would be unwilling to accept such an offer. The farmers therefore would not cultivate the land. The outcome, once again, would be the same whatever the legal position. Furthermore, the outcome would be such as maximized the value of production. Assume the rents of the ranchers were $40, the value of crops destroyed $50, and the rents of the farmers $30. If both ranchers and farmers continued to operate, the increase in the value of production over what it would otherwise be would be $20 ($40 plus $30 minus $50). If the farmers alone continued to operate, the increase would be $30 (the rents of the farmers) while if the ranchers alone continued to operate, the increase would be $40 (the rents of the ranchers).

Finally, we may consider the case in which the value of the damage to the crops is greater than the rents of either the farmers or the ranchers, but the rents of the farmers are greater than the rents of the ranchers. Assume first that the ranchers are liable for crop damage. In this case the ranchers would be unable to compensate the farmers for crop destruction and continue their operations. They would also be unable to induce the farmers to cease cultivation, since the maximum the ranchers could pay is slightly less than their own rents, while the farmers would not be willing to cease cultivation unless they received slightly more than their own rents (which are greater than the ranchers' rents). Assume now that the ranchers are not liable for the damage. In these circumstances, the farmers

169

could avoid the damage (whose continuation would force them to abandon cultivation) by making a payment which was greater than the ranchers' rents to induce them to move to their best alternative (and therefore stop the crop damage). This the farmers could do and still be better off than if they ceased to cultivate their crops, given that the farmers' rents are greater than the ranchers' rents. Whatever the rule of liability, the result would be that the farmers would continue to cultivate their land while the ranchers would not engage in cattle raising. A calculation similar to that in the immediately preceding example would also demonstrate that this allocation of resources was such as maximized the value of production.

The examination of all these cases has been tedious, but the results are conclusive. The allocation of resources remains the same in all circumstances, whatever the legal position. Furthermore, the result in each case maximizes the value of production as measured on the market, that is, it maximizes the sum of the ranchers' rents and the farmers' rents minus the value of the crops destroyed. Damage to crops will only persist if it is less in value than the rents of both the ranchers and the farmers. If damage is greater than the rents of either the ranchers or the farmers, but not of both, the activity in which rents are less than the damage will not be undertaken. And if damage is greater than the rents of both the ranchers and the farmers, the activity will not take place which yields the lower rent. Whatever the circumstances, the value of total production will be maximized. These results would remain essentially unchanged if, instead of the question being solely whether there would be ranching or not or farming or not, it had also allowed for the possibility that there could be more or less cattle raising and more or less cultivation of crops, but the calculations would have been even more tedious.

IV. The Assignment of Rights and the Distribution of Wealth

In section III of these notes it was demonstrated that, in a regime of zero transaction costs, the allocation of resources remains the same whatever the legal position regarding liability for harmful effects. However, many economists have argued that this conclusion is wrong, since, even in a regime of zero transaction costs, a change in the legal position affects the distribution of wealth. This will lead to alterations in the demands for goods and services, including—and this is the heart of the matter—those produced by the activity generating the harmful effects and those produced by the activities affected by them. Thus, if we return to the example of the previous section, it would appear that the farmers are always better off and the ranchers worse off if the ranchers are made liable for the damage brought about by their cattle than if they are not. If the ranchers are made liable, they pay the farmers a sum of money to compensate them for the damage, or they pay them not to produce (so there is no damage), or they avoid creating damage by not ranching and choosing instead to work in their next best employment, in which case they receive a lower income. When there is no liability for damage, the farmers receive no compensation when there is damage and continue farming with a reduced income, or they themselves have to pay the ranchers not to operate (so that there is no damage), or they move to their next best employment and receive a lower income. These changes in the wealth of the ranchers and farmers will lead, it is said, to changes in their demands and will thus bring about a change in the allocation of resources.

I consider this argument to be wrong, since a change in the liability rule will not lead to any alteration in the distribution of wealth. There are therefore no subsequent effects on demands to be taken into account. Let us see why. In section III of these notes, I spoke of the group of factors engaged in ranching as "ranchers" and the group of factors engaged in farming as "farmers." Let us separate the group of factors called "ranchers" into ranchers and ranching land and the group of factors called "farmers" into farmers and farming land, and let us furthermore make the perhaps not very unrealistic assumption that only the ranching land and the farming land earn "rents" as defined in section III. Assume also that the land is leased by the ranchers and farmers.

Let us confine ourselves to the simple case in which the damage inflicted by the cattle is less than the "rents" of either the ranching land or the farming land. Consider the effect of the rule of liability on the terms of the contracts entered into by those engaged in ranching and farming. If the rancher has to compensate the farmer for the damage inflicted by his cattle, the amount he would pay for leasing the land would be lower by the sum he would have to pay as compensation than it would be if he did not have to make such a payment, while the farmer would pay a price for leasing his land higher by the same sum than he would if he did not receive any compensation for damage. The wealth of the ranchers and farmers would remain the same whatever the legal position regarding liability for the damage inflicted by the cattle. But what of the land-owners? If compensation has to be paid for damage to crops, the price for leasing the ranching land will be less, and that for the farming land will be more than if compensation does not have to be paid. However, if the rule of liability is known, the amount that will have been paid to acquire the land will reflect this, less being paid for the ranching land and more for the farming land when compensation has to be paid than when it does not have to be paid. The wealth of the land-owners would thus remain the same, changes in the amount paid for the land offsetting the changes in the flow of payments brought about by a difference in the legal position regarding liability for damage. There is no change in the distribution of wealth associated with the choice of a different legal rule and therefore no subsequent changes in demand, the effects of which need to be taken into account. While I have only considered the case in which damage was less than the "rents" of both the ranching land and the farming land, a similar argument would lead to the same conclusion in all the cases discussed in section III.

It may be thought that this analysis of the effects of a difference in the legal position, if it is assumed in each case that all parties are fully adjusted to it, is not applicable when there is a change from one rule of law to another. This is not so. The conclusion that there will be no redistribution of wealth when there are zero transaction costs is unaffected, although this result is reached by a somewhat different route. Remember that with zero transaction costs it costs nothing to make a contract more elaborate. Given that this is so, contracts would be drawn up specifying how payments were to vary with changes in the legal position. In the example we have just discussed, it would be provided that if, for example, the rule of law changed from one in which the ranchers were not liable for the damage inflicted by their cattle to one in which they were liable, the amount which the ranchers would pay for the lease of their land would decrease and owners of ranching land would receive a rebate from those from whom they bought the land, while farmers would have to pay more for the lease of their land and owners of farming land would be required to make an additional payment to those from whom they bought the land. The distribution of wealth would remain the same.

Whether a difference in the law will affect the allocation of resources is not so easily settled in the case of previously unrecognized rights. Different criteria for assigning ownership of these rights would seem in this case to lead inevitably to a different distribution of wealth. It might, of course, be argued that since, with zero transaction costs, it costs nothing to make a contract more elaborate, all contingencies will be provided for and therefore no redistribution of wealth could occur. But it would be unreasonable to assume that people could include in contracts a reference to rights of which they were unable to conceive. The question which then has to be considered is whether, through its influence on demand, a change in the criteria for assigning ownership to previously unrecognized rights could bring about a different allocation of resources. I first advanced the proposition now known as the "Coase Theorem" in my article on "The Federal Communications Commission." As was explained earlier, the example used to illustrate my argument concerned the ownership of a newly discovered cave. I concluded: "Whether the cave is used for storing bank records, as a natural gas reservoir, or for growing mushrooms depends, not on the law of property, but on whether the bank, the natural gas corporation, or the mushroom concern will pay the most in order to be able to use the cave."[15] It never entered my head to add the qualification that if the demand for mushrooms of the possible claimants to the cave differed and if their expenditure on mushrooms (or banking

15. Coase, "Federal Communications Commission," 25.

services or natural gas) was an important item in their budgets, and if their consumption of these products was a significant part of total consumption, the decision concerning ownership of a newly discovered cave would affect the demand for banking services, natural gas, and mushrooms. As a result the relative prices of banking services, natural gas, and mushrooms would change; such a change might affect the amount which the various businesses concerned would be willing to pay for the use of the cave, and this might possibly affect the way in which the cave was used. It cannot be denied that it is conceivable that a change in the criteria for assigning ownership to previously unrecognized rights may lead to changes in demand which in turn lead to a difference in the allocation of resources, but, apart from such cataclysmic events as the abolition of slavery, these effects will normally be so insignificant that they can safely be neglected. This is also true of those changes in the distribution of wealth which accompany a change in the law when there are positive transaction costs and it is too costly for the contracts to cover all contingencies. Thus, in considering the legal case of *Sturges v. Bridgman*, it may well be, given the form of the contracts into which they had entered, that the legal decision affected the relative wealth of the doctor and confectioner (and perhaps had similar effects on the wealth of those occupying neighbouring premises), but it is inconceivable to me that this could have any noticeable effect on the demand for cakes or medical services.

V. The Influence of Transaction Costs

The world of zero transaction costs has often been described as a Coasian world. Nothing could be further from the truth. It is the world of modern economic theory, one which I was hoping to persuade economists to leave. What I did in "The Problem of Social Cost" was simply to bring to light some of its properties. I argued that in such a world the allocation of resources would be independent of the legal position, a result which Stigler dubbed the "Coase Theorem": ". . . under perfect competition private and social costs will be equal."[16] For

16. Stigler, *Theory of Price*, 113.

reasons given earlier, it would seem that even the qualifying phrase "under perfect competition" can be omitted. Economists, following Pigou whose work has dominated thought in this area, have consequently been engaged in an attempt to explain why there were divergences between private and social costs and what should be done about it, using a theory in which private and social costs were necessarily always equal. It is therefore hardly surprising that the conclusions reached were often incorrect. The reason why economists went wrong was that their theoretical system did not take into account a factor which is essential if one wishes to analyze the effect of a change in the law on the allocation of resources. This missing factor is the existence of transaction costs.

With zero transaction costs, producers would make whatever set of contractual arrangements was necessary to maximize the value of production. If there were actions that could be taken which cost less than the reduction in damage that they would bring, and they were the least costly means available to accomplish such a reduction, they would be undertaken. Action might be required by a single producer or by several in combination. As I indicated in "The Problem of Social Cost" in discussing the cattle-crop example, these measures include such actions as, for the farmer, taking all or part of the crop-land out of cultivation or planting another crop less susceptible to damage; for the rancher, reducing the size of the herd or the kind of cattle raised, or employing herdsmen or dogs, or tethering the cattle; or, on the part of either the farmer or the rancher, the erection of fencing. One can even imagine more unusual measures, such as the farmer keeping a pet tiger whose scent would suffice to keep the cattle away from the crops. Both the farmer and the rancher would have an incentive to employ any measure known to them (including joint actions) which would raise the value of production, since each producer would share in the resulting increase in income.

However, once transaction costs are taken into account, many of these measures will not be undertaken because making the contractual arrangements necessary to bring them into existence would cost more than the gain they make possible. To simplify the discussion, assume that *all* contractual arrangements aimed at reducing the amount of damage are too costly. The result would be, in our example, that if the ranchers are liable to pay compensation for the damage caused by their cattle, the farmers would have no reason to modify their arrangements, since compensation for crops damaged or destroyed would always substitute for sale on the market. The ranchers, however, are in a different position. They have an incentive to change their mode of operating whenever this raises their costs by an amount which is less than the resulting reduction in the compensation paid to the farmers. Suppose, however, that the ranchers are not liable. They now have no incentive to change their arrangements. It is the farmers who will take steps to reduce damage when the gain from the additional crops that become available for sale exceeds the cost incurred to bring this result about. It is easy to show that, in these circumstances, the value of production may be greater if the ranchers are not made liable for the damage to the crops caused by their cattle than if they are. Assume that, if the ranchers were liable, they would find it in their interest to take steps which would completely eliminate the damage, and that the farmers would take action with the same effect if the ranchers were not liable. Assume further that the cost of eliminating the damage is $80 for the ranchers and $50 for the farmers. If the ranchers were not liable, it will be the farmers who take steps to eliminate the damage. The cost to them would be $50. Had the ranchers been liable for the crop damage brought about by their cattle, they would have done what was necessary to eliminate the damage. The cost to them would have been $80. It follows that the value of production is greater by $30 ($80 − $50) if the ranchers are not liable. The purpose of this illustration is not to suggest that those generating harmful effects should never be made liable to compensate those harmed. By interchanging the costs of eliminating the damage for the ranchers and farmers, we would have an example of a situation in which the value of production would be greater if the ranchers were made liable for the damage brought about by their cattle. What these examples show is that whether the value of production will be greater when the ranchers are liable or when they are not liable depends on the circumstances of the particular case.

It has been suggested that my argument needs modification to take account of the fact that, at least in common law countries, damages must be mitigated. I assumed that the ranchers, if not liable, and the farmers, if the ranchers were liable, had no incentive to incur costs to reduce damage. It has been pointed out that, in common law countries, to collect compensation for damage when the ranchers are liable, the farmers must take reasonable steps to mitigate the damage, while the ranchers, if they are not liable, must do the same thing if they are to avoid a claim against them. This is no doubt important for those engaged in analyzing the working of a common law system, but it does not change the point that I was making.

While the existence of such a doctrine may lead the ranchers and the farmers to undertake some expenditures which otherwise they would not, the courts are not likely to consider that such expenditures should be incurred unless it is abundantly clear that they would reduce damage by a greater amount, and, what is just as important, that the actions required to bring about this reduction in damage are known to them. It is impossible for me to believe that the doctrine of mitigation of damages would lead the ranchers to take all the measures to reduce damage that they would take if they were liable to compensate the farmers, or that it would lead the farmers to take all the measures to reduce damage that they would take if the ranchers were not liable. If this is true, my conclusion is unaffected. If, after the mitigation of damages, the ranchers would have to incur costs of $70 to eliminate the damage (the remaining damage being more than $70) and the farmers could do this for $20, the value of production would clearly be greater by $50 if the ranchers were not liable for damage and it was therefore the farmers who were forced to take action to prevent the damage. Of course, with other figures a situation could be created in which the value of production would be greater if the ranchers were liable.

It has also been suggested by Zerbe that my conclusion is incorrect because the liability rule which I use in my analysis is not optimal.[17] This objection is based on a misunderstanding of the character of my argument, which is that, in the presence of transaction costs, the liability rule cannot be optimal. In a zero transaction cost world in which all parties have an incentive to discover and disclose all those adjustments which would have the effect of increasing the value of production, the information needed to calculate the optimal liability rule can be imagined to be available, although it would also be superfluous since, in these circumstances, the value of production would be maximized whatever the rule of liability. But once we take transaction costs into account, the various parties have no incentive (or a reduced incentive) to disclose the information needed to formulate an optimal liability rule. Indeed, this information may not even be known to them, since those who have no incentive to disclose information have no reason for discovering what it is. Information needed for transactions which cannot be carried out will not be collected.

The same approach which, with zero transaction costs, demonstrates that the allocation of resources remains the same whatever the legal position, also shows that, with positive transaction costs, the law plays a crucial role in determining how resources are used. But it does more than this. With zero transaction costs, the same result is reached because contractual arrangements will be made to modify the rights and duties of the parties so as to make it in their interest to undertake those actions which maximize the value of production. With positive transaction costs, some or all of these contractual arrangements become too costly to carry out. The incentives to take some of the actions which would have maximized the value of production disappear. What incentives will be lacking depends on what the law is, since this determines what contractual arrangements will have to be made to bring about those actions which maximize the value of production. The result brought about by different legal rules is not intuitively obvious and depends on the facts of each particular case. It may be, for example, as was shown earlier in this section, that the value

17. Richard O. Zerbe, Jr., "The Problem of Social Cost: Fifteen Years Later," in *Theory and Measurement of Economic Externalities*, 33.

of production will be greater if those generating harmful effects are not liable to compensate those who suffer the harm they cause.

VI. Pigovian Taxes

Up to the time of the publication of "The Problem of Social Cost," the effect of different liability rules on the allocation of resources was very little discussed in the economics literature. Economists, following Pigou, spoke of uncompensated disservices and implied that those responsible for these harmful effects ought to be liable to compensate those they harmed, but the subject of liability rules was not something to which economists gave much attention. Most economists have thought that the problems arising from the producers' actions which had harmful effects on others were best handled by instituting an appropriate system of taxes and subsidies, with the emphasis being placed on the use of taxes. Thus, in the introduction to a recent article it is said: "It is an established result of economic theory that the achievement of efficiency in a competitive economy requires taxes (subsidies) on commodities generating negative (positive) economic effects."[18] Whatever its merits as a means of regulating the generation of harmful effects, the use of taxes had the added attraction that it could be analyzed by existing price theory, that the schemes devised looked impressive on a blackboard or in articles, and that it required no knowledge of the subject.

I argued towards the end of my article on "The Problem of Social Cost" that a taxing system could not be assumed to produce an optimal allocation of resources, even if the authorities wished to do so. My argument, however, was apparently not well expressed, since even as sympathetic a critic as Baumol failed to understand it. Baumol's criticisms were directed at a position that I did not, and do not, hold. What I will therefore do is to set out my argument more clearly, expanding on those points in which compression or poor exposition may have led my critics astray. Many of those who have

18. Agnar Sandmo, "Anomaly and Stability in the Theory of Externalities," *Quarterly Journal of Economics* 94, no. 4 (June 1980): 799.

written on the use of taxation to deal with harmful effects have accepted Baumol's interpretation of my argument, but confining my comments to Baumol's contribution will be enough to make my own position clear.[19]

I started my argument by saying that I was assuming that the tax would equal the value of the damage caused. The example I used to illustrate my argument was that of a factory whose smoke would cause damage of $100 per annum but in which a smoke-prevention device could be installed for $90. Since emitting smoke would involve the owner of the factory in paying taxes of $100, he would install the smoke-prevention device, thereby saving $10 per annum. Nevertheless the situation may not be optimal. Assume that those who would suffer the damage could avoid it by taking steps which would cost $40 per annum. In this case, if there were no tax and the factory emitted the smoke, the value of production would be greater by $50 per annum ($90 minus $40). Later I noted that an increase in the number of people or businesses locating near the factory would increase the amount of damage produced by a given emission of smoke. This would result in higher taxes if the smoke emissions continued, and consequently the factory would be willing to incur greater costs for smoke prevention than it would previously in order to avoid paying the higher taxes. Those deciding to locate near the factory would not take into account these additional costs. This is easily illustrated using the same figures. Suppose initially that no one was located near the factory. There would be smoke but no damage, and therefore no taxes. Now suppose that a developer decides to build a new subdivision in the vicinity of the factory and that in consequence the value of the damage occasioned by the smoke becomes $100 per annum. The developer could count on the factory-owner installing the smoke-prevention device costing $90 per annum, since this would enable him to avoid a tax of $100. Those settling near the factory will not suffer any damage from smoke, which will not now exist. But the situation may not be optimal. The developer might have been

19. William J. Baumol, "On Taxation and the Control of Externalities," *American Economic Review* 62, no. 3 (June 1972): 307–22.

able to choose another location equally satisfactory and without smoke for an additional cost of $40 per annum. Once again, the value of production would have been greater by $50 per annum if there had been no tax and the factory had continued to emit its smoke.

I also said that if "the factory-owner is to be made to pay a tax equal to the damage caused, it would clearly be desirable to institute a double tax system and to make residents of the district pay an amount equal to the additional cost incurred by the factory-owner . . . in order to avoid the damage."[20] This is easily shown. The additional cost that would be incurred by the factory-owner in our example is $90 per annum. Assume that a tax of $90 is laid on the residents of the subdivision. In this case the developer would prefer to build his subdivision elsewhere, incurring an additional cost of $40 per annum but avoiding the tax of $90 per annum, with the result that the factory would continue to emit smoke and the value of production would be maximized.

It would be wrong to conclude that I was advocating the introduction of a double tax system or indeed any tax system for that matter. I merely pointed out that if there is a tax based on *damage*, it would also be desirable to tax those whose presence imposes costs on the firm responsible for the harmful effects. But as I said in "The Problem of Social Cost," any tax system bristles with difficulties and what is desirable may be impossible.

Baumol, who discussed my views at length in his article, said that his main purpose was "to show that, taken on its own grounds, the conclusions of the Pigovian tradition are, in fact, impeccable."[21] He argues that, in the case of the smoke nuisance, an "appropriately chosen tax, levied only on the factory (without payment of compensation to local residents) is precisely what is needed for optimal resource allocation under pure competition."[22] He argued further that a double tax (such as I suggested) is unnecessary and claimed that my belief that

20. See "The Problem of Social Cost," 151–52.
21. Baumol, "On Taxation," 307.
22. Ibid., 309.

a taxing system could result in too many people locating near the factory comes from confusing a pecuniary externality with a technological externality. An examination of my arithmetic earlier in this section will, however, demonstrate that my conclusions are correct. Why do Baumol and I reach different answers? The reason is that in my article I assumed that the tax which is to be imposed is equal to the *damage caused*, whereas Baumol's tax is not. I would not deny that Baumol's taxing system is conceivable and that if put into practice it would have the results he describes. My objection, which I stated in my article, is that it could not be put into practice. I thought I had made this clear. This is what I said in "The Problem of Social Cost": "A tax system which was confined to a tax on the producer for damage caused would tend to lead to unduly high costs being incurred for the prevention of damage. Of course, this could be avoided if it were possible to base the tax, not on the damage caused, but on the fall in the value of production (in its widest sense) resulting from the emission of smoke. But to do so would require a detailed knowledge of individual preferences, and I am unable to imagine how the data needed for such a taxation system could be assembled."[23]

What I had in mind becomes clear if we consider how the Pigovian tax scheme would be implemented. Note that it is intended to apply, as Baumol points out, to the "large numbers" case. In our example, therefore, many people and/or businesses must be presumed to be affected by the smoke from the factory. Note also that none of the tax receipts is to be given as compensation to those harmed by the smoke. They would thus have an incentive to adopt measures which reduce the value of damage whenever they could do so at a lower cost. The costs of such measures, together with the value of the remaining damage, would be calculated and totalled for all those affected (or who might be affected) by the smoke. A new calculation would have to be made for each level of smoke emission, or at least for enough of them so that a schedule could be drawn up showing the fall in the value of production resulting from the smoke for each level of smoke emission.

23. See "The Problem of Social Cost," 152.

The tax would be set for each level of smoke emission equal to the fall in value of production which it brought about. The factory-owner would then be presented with this schedule and he would choose his method of production and the amount of smoke that would be emitted, taking into account the taxes that he would have to pay. He would reduce smoke emission whenever the additional costs he would incur to do this were less than the taxes that would be saved. Since the tax is equal to the fall in the value of production elsewhere occasioned by the smoke, and the increased costs due to the change in methods represents the fall in the value of production in the smoke-producing activity, the factory-owner, in choosing whether to incur additional costs or pay the tax, would make that decision which maximizes the value of production. It is in this sense that the tax system may be said to be optimal.

The position is, however, much more complicated than this. The factory-owner would not normally wish to conduct his business in such a way that the level of smoke emission remained constant over time, but would wish to operate in a way which resulted in variations in the amount of smoke emitted. The extent and timing of these fluctuations in smoke emission would affect the adjustments that those in the vicinity of the factory would find it profitable to make. There is an infinite number of possible patterns of smoke emission, but no doubt it would be thought sufficient to obtain from those in the vicinity of the factory (or those elsewhere who might settle there) what their responses would be to a somewhat smaller number of patterns of smoke emission in order to procure the data from which to devise an appropriate taxing scheme. Of course, as the measures which it would be profitable to take to offset the effects of the smoke emissions would depend on their duration, data would need to be gathered for many years into the future.

As is obvious, even this is a highly simplified account of a very complicated process, but it gives some idea of what would have to be done to implement the Pigovian tax scheme. All those in the area affected by the smoke (or an adequate sample of them) would have to disclose what damage they would suffer from the smoke, what steps they would take to avoid or reduce the damage, and what it would cost them with different patterns of smoke emission from the factory. Similar enquiries would also have to be made of those not in the area but who might come into it if the level of smoke emission were reduced sufficiently (we must assume, of course, that they could be identified). The information which is being sought from this large number of people is information which, if they possessed it, they could have no interest in disclosing and which, for the most part, they would not know. There is, as I see it, no way in which the information required for the Pigovian tax scheme could be collected.

The tax system which I discussed in "The Problem of Social Cost" was one in which the tax was equal to the damage caused. While this requires much less information to be collected than is needed for the Pigovian tax scheme, it cannot easily be obtained and, in any case, as I explained, the results obtained are not optimal. My main purpose was to show this. I added that if the factory-owner has to pay a tax based on damage, it would also be desirable to make those who would suffer the damage from the smoke pay a tax equal to the costs incurred by the factory-owner to avoid causing the damage. My reason was that if the tax is based on damage, it could be that people and businesses would establish themselves in the vicinity of the factory and in consequence the factory-owner would install smoke-prevention devices even though the cost would be lower if those situated near the factory chose another location. Baumol argues that this would not happen because "the externalities (the smoke) keep down the size of the nearby population."[24] However, he assumes that the Pigovian tax system is in operation, which is not what I was assuming. The tax system I was discussing was one in which the tax was based on damage. With this tax system, the factory-owner has an incentive to install a smoke-prevention device in circumstances which would not exist with the Pigovian tax scheme. Once the smoke-prevention device is installed, there would be no smoke and therefore nothing to deter those who wish to locate near the factory; and given the amount of damage, they can count on the smoke-prevention device being installed. The object of

24. Baumol, "On Taxation," 312.

the double tax would be to deter people and businesses from locating near the factory and adding to its costs when it would be less costly if they located somewhere else. However, I do not wish to debate the relative merits of these various tax systems which would take us into a thicket of complicated argumentation and, so far as I am concerned, to no purpose. All these tax systems have extremely serious flaws and would certainly not produce results which economists would consider to be optimal. Whether some tax system, however defective, might, in some circumstances, be better than any alternative (including inaction) is another matter, and on this I express no opinion.

Later in his article, Baumol makes what is essentially the same point. He says: "All in all, we are left with little reason for confidence in the applicability of the Pigovian approach, literally interpreted. We do not know how to calculate the required taxes and subsidies and we do not know how to approximate them by trial and error."[25] Apparently what Baumol meant by saying that, "taken on its own grounds, the conclusions of the Pigovian tradition are, in fact, impeccable," was that its logic was impeccable and that, if its taxation proposals were carried out, which they cannot be, the allocation of resources would be optimal. This I have never denied. My point was simply that such tax proposals are the stuff that dreams are made of. In my youth it was said that what was too silly to be said may be sung. In modern economics it may be put into mathematics.

25. Ibid., 318.

SEVEN

The Lighthouse in Economics

I. Introduction

The lighthouse appears in the writings of economists because of the light it is supposed to throw on the question of the economic functions of government. It is often used as an example of something which has to be provided by government rather than by private enterprise. What economists usually seem to have in mind is that the impossibility of securing payment from the owners of the ships that benefit from the existence of the lighthouse makes it unprofitable for any private individual or firm to build and maintain a lighthouse.

John Stuart Mill in his *Principles of Political Economy,* in the chapter "Of the Grounds and Limits of the Laissez-Faire or Non-Interference Principle," said:

> . . . it is a proper office of government to build and maintain lighthouses, establish buoys, etc. for the security of navigation: for since it is impossible that the ships at sea which are benefited by a lighthouse, should be made to pay a toll on the occasion of its use, no one would build lighthouses from motives of personal

Reprinted from *The Journal of Law and Economics* 17, no. 2 (October 1974): 357–76. ©1974 by The University of Chicago Press. All rights reserved.

It is with great pleasure that I acknowledge the helpfulness of members of Trinity House and of officials in the Department of Trade and of the Chamber of Shipping in providing me with information on the British lighthouse system. They are not, however, in any way responsible for the use I have made of this information and should not be presumed to share the conclusions I draw.

interest, unless indemnified and rewarded from a compulsory levy made by the state.[1]

Henry Sidgwick in his *Principles of Political Economy,* in the chapter "The System of Natural Liberty Considered in Relation to Production," had this to say:

> . . . there is a large and varied class of cases in which the supposition [that an individual can always obtain through free *exchange* adequate remuneration for the services he renders] would be manifestly erroneous. In the first place there are some utilities which, from their nature, are practically incapable of being appropriated by those who produce them or would be willing to purchase them. For instance, it may easily happen that the benefits of a well-placed lighthouse must be largely enjoyed by ships on which no toll could be conveniently imposed.[2]

Pigou in *The Economics of Welfare* used Sidgwick's lighthouse example as an instance of uncompensated services, in which "marginal net product falls short of marginal social net product, because incidental services are performed to third parties from whom it is technically difficult to exact payment."[3]

Paul A. Samuelson, in his *Economics,* is more forthright than these earlier writers. In the section on the "Economic Role of Government," he says that "government provides certain indispensable *public* services without which community life would be unthinkable and which by their nature cannot appropriately be left to private enterprise." He gives as "obvious examples" the maintenance of national defense and of

1. John Stuart Mill, *Principles of Political Economy,* vol. 3 of *The Collected Works of John Stuart Mill,* ed. J. M. Robson (Toronto: University of Toronto Press, 1965), 968.

2. Henry Sidgwick, *The Principles of Political Economy,* 3rd ed. (London: Macmillan & Co., 1901), 406. In the first edition (1883), the sentence relating to lighthouses is the same but the rest of the wording (but not the sense) is somewhat changed.

3. A. C. Pigou, *The Economics of Welfare,* 4th ed. (London: Macmillan & Co., 1932), 183–84.

internal law and order, and the administration of justice and of contracts, and he adds in a footnote:

> Here is a later example of government service: light-houses. These save lives and cargoes; but lighthouse keepers cannot reach out to collect fees from skippers. "So," says the advanced treatise, "we have here a divergence between *private* advantage and money cost [as seen by a man odd enough to try to make his fortune running a lighthouse business] and true *social* advantage and cost [as measured by lives and cargoes saved in comparison with (1) total costs of the lighthouse and (2) extra costs that result from letting one more ship look at the warning light]." Philosophers and statesmen have always recognized the necessary role of government in such cases of "external-economy divergence between private and social advantage."[4]

Later Samuelson again refers to the lighthouse as a "government activit[y] justifiable because of external effects." He says:

> Take our earlier case of a lighthouse to warn against rocks. Its beam helps everyone in sight. A businessman could not build it for a profit, since he cannot claim a price from each user. This certainly is the kind of activity that governments would naturally undertake.[5]

Samuelson does not leave the matter here. He also uses the lighthouse to make another point (one not found in the earlier writers). He says:

> . . . in the lighthouse example one thing should be noticed: The fact that the lighthouse operators cannot appropriate in the form of a purchase price a fee from those it benefits certainly helps to make it a suitable social or public good. But even if the operators were

4. P. A. Samuelson, *Economics: An Introductory Analysis,* 6th ed. (New York: McGraw-Hill, 1964). All references to Samuelson's *Economics* will be to the 6th edition.
5. Samuelson, *Economics,* 159.

able—say, by radar reconnaisance—to claim a toll from every nearby user, that fact would not necessarily make it socially optimal for this service to be provided like a private good at a market-determined individual price. Why not? Because it costs society *zero extra cost* to let one extra ship use the service; hence any ships discouraged from those waters by the requirement to pay a positive price will represent a social economic loss—even if the price charged to all is no more than enough to pay the long-run expenses of the lighthouse. If the lighthouse is socially worth building and operating—and it need not be—a more advanced treatise can show how this social good is worth being made optimally available to all.[6]

There is an element of paradox in Samuelson's position. The government has to provide lighthouses because private firms could not charge for their services. But if it were possible for private firms to make such a charge they should not be allowed to do so (which also presumably calls for government action). Samuelson's position is quite different from that of Mill, Sidgwick, or Pigou. As I read these writers, the difficulty of charging for the use of a lighthouse is a serious point with important consequences for lighthouse policy. They had no objection to charging as such and therefore, if this were possible, to the private operation of lighthouses. Mill's argument is not, however, free from ambiguity. He argues that the government should build and maintain lighthouses because, since ships benefitted cannot be made to pay a toll, private enterprise would not provide a lighthouse service. But he then adds the qualifying phrase "unless indemnified and rewarded from a compulsory levy made by the state." I take a "compulsory levy" to be one imposed on ships benefitted by the lighthouse (the levy would be, in effect, a toll). The element of ambiguity in Mill's exposition is whether he meant that the "compulsory levy" would make it possible for people to "build lighthouses from motives of personal interest" and therefore for governmental operation to be avoided, or whether he meant that it

6. Ibid., 151.

was not possible (or desirable) for private firms to be "indemnified and rewarded from a compulsory levy" and that therefore governmental operation was required. My own opinion is that Mill had in mind the first of these alternative interpretations and, if this is right, it represents an important qualification to his view that building and maintaining lighthouses is "a proper office of the government." In any case, it seems clear that Mill had no objection in principle to the imposition of tolls.[7] Sidgwick's point (to which Pigou refers) raises no problems of interpretation. It is, however, very restricted in character. He says that "it may easily happen that the benefits of a well-placed lighthouse must be largely enjoyed by ships on which no toll could be conveniently imposed." This does not say that charging is impossible: indeed, it implies the contrary. What it says is that there may be circumstances in which most of those who benefit from the lighthouse can avoid paying the toll. It does not say that there may not be circumstances in which the benefits of the lighthouse are largely enjoyed by ships on which a toll could be conveniently laid and it implies that, in these circumstances, it would be desirable to impose a toll—which would make private operation of lighthouses possible.

It is, I think, difficult to understand exactly what Mill, Sidgwick, and Pigou meant without some knowledge of the British lighthouse system since, although these writers were probably unfamiliar with how the British system operated in detail, they were doubtless aware of its general character and this must have been in the back of their minds when they wrote about lighthouses. However, knowledge of the British lighthouse system not only enables one to have a greater understanding of Mill, Sidgwick, and Pigou; it also provides a context within which to appraise Samuelson's statements about lighthouses.

II. The British Lighthouse System

The authorities in Britain which build and maintain lighthouses are Trinity House (for England and Wales), the Commissioners

7. Compare what Mill has to say on tolls in *Principles of Political Economy*, 862–63.

of Northern Lighthouses (for Scotland), and the Commissioners of Irish Lights (for Ireland). The expenses of these authorities are met out of the General Lighthouse Fund. The income of this Fund is derived from light dues, which are paid by shipowners. The responsibility for making the arrangements for payment of the light dues and for maintaining the accounts is placed on Trinity House (whether the payments are made in England, Wales, Scotland, or Ireland), although the actual collection is made by the customs authorities at the ports. The money obtained from the light dues is paid into the General Lighthouse Fund, which is under the control of the Department of Trade. The lighthouse authorities draw on the General Lighthouse Fund to meet their expenditures.

The relation of the Department of Trade to the various lighthouse authorities is somewhat similar to that of the Treasury to a British Government Department. The budgets of the authorities have to be approved by the Department. The proposed budgets of the three authorities are submitted about Christmas time and are discussed at a Lighthouse Conference held annually in London. In addition to the three lighthouse authorities and the Department, there are also present at the conference members of the Lights Advisory Committee, a committee of the Chamber of Shipping (a trade association) representing shipowners, underwriters, and shippers. The Lights Advisory Committee, although without statutory authority, plays an important part in the review procedure, and the opinions it expresses are taken into account both by the lighthouse authorities in drawing up their budgets and by the Department in deciding on whether to approve the budgets. The light dues are set by the Department at a level which will yield, over a period of years, an amount of money sufficient to meet the likely expenditures. But in deciding on the program of works and changes in existing arrangements, the participants in the conference, particularly the members of the Lights Advisory Committee, have regard to the effect which new works or changes in existing arrangements would have on the level of light dues.

The basis on which light dues are levied was set out in the Second Schedule to the Merchant Shipping (Mercantile Marine

Fund) Act of 1898.[8] Modifications to the level of the dues and to certain other respects have been made since then by Order in Council but the present method of charging is essentially that established in 1898. The dues are so much per net ton payable per voyage for all vessels arriving at, or departing from, ports in Britain. In the case of "Home Trade" ships, there is no further liability for light dues after the first 10 voyages in a year, and in the case of "Foreign-going" ships there is no further liability after 6 voyages. The light dues are different for these two categories of ship and are such that, for a ship of given size, 10 voyages for a "Home Trade" ship yield approximately the same sum as 6 voyages for a "Foreign-going" ship. Some categories of ship pay at a lower rate per net ton: sailing vessels of more than 100 tons and cruise ships. Tugs and pleasure yachts make an annual payment rather than a payment per voyage. In addition, some ships are exempt from light dues: ships belonging to the British or Foreign Governments (unless carrying cargo or passengers for remuneration), fishing vessels, hoppers and dredges, sailing vessels (except pleasure yachts) of less than 100 tons, all ships (including pleasure yachts) of less than 20 tons, vessels (other than tugs or pleasure yachts) in ballast, or those putting in for bunker fuel or stores or because of the hazards of the sea. All these statements are subject to qualification. But they make clear the general nature of the scheme.

The present position is that the expenses of the British lighthouse service are met out of the General Lighthouse Fund, the income of which comes from light dues. In addition to expenditures on lighthouses in Great Britain and Ireland, the Fund is also used to pay for the maintenance of some colonial lighthouses and to meet the cost of marking and clearing wrecks (to the extent that these are not reimbursed by a salvaging firm), although these payments amount to only a very small proportion of total expenditures. There are also expenditures on lighthouses which are not met out of the Fund. The expenses of building and maintaining "local lights," those which are only of benefit to ships using particular ports, are not paid for out

8. 61 & 62 Vict. ch. 44, sched. 2.

of the Fund, which is restricted to the finance of lighthouses which are useful for "general navigation." The expenditures for "local lights" are normally made by harbour authorities and are recovered out of port dues.

III. The Evolution of the British Lighthouse System

Mill, writing in 1848, and Sidgwick, in 1883, to the extent that they had in mind the actual British lighthouse system, would obviously be thinking of earlier arrangements. To understand Mill and Sidgwick, we need to know something of the lighthouse system in the nineteenth century and of the way in which it had evolved. But a study of the history of the British lighthouse system is not only useful because it helps us to understand Mill and Sidgwick, but also because it serves to enlarge our vision of the range of alternative institutional arrangements available for operating a lighthouse service. In discussing the history of the British lighthouse service, I will confine myself to England and Wales, which is, presumably, the part of the system with which Mill and Sidgwick would have been most familiar.

The principal lighthouse authority in England and Wales is Trinity House. It is also the principal pilotage authority for the United Kingdom. It maintains Homes and administers charitable trusts for mariners and their wives, widows, and orphans. It has also many miscellaneous responsibilities, for example, the inspection and regulation of "local lights" and the provision of Nautical Assessors or Trinity Masters at the hearing of marine cases in the Law Courts. It is represented on a number of harbour boards, including the Port of London Authority, and members of Trinity House serve on many committees (including government committees) dealing with maritime matters.

Trinity House is an ancient institution. It seems to have evolved out of a medieval seamen's guild. A petition asking for incorporation was presented to Henry VIII in 1513 and letters patent were granted in 1514.[9] The charter gave Trinity

---

9. G. G. Harris, *Trinity House of Deptford 1515–1660* (London: Athlone Press, 1969), 19–20. My sketch of the early history of Trinity House is largely based on this work, particularly ch. 7, "Beacons, Markes and Signes for the Sea" and ch. 8, "An Uncertaine Light."

House the right to regulate pilotage, and this, together with its charitable work, represented its main activity for many years. It did not concern itself with lighthouses until much later.

There seem to have been few lighthouses in Britain before the seventeenth century and not many until the eighteenth century. There were, however, seamarks of various kinds. Most of these were on land and were not designed as aids to mariners, consisting of church steeples, houses, clumps of trees, etc. Buoys and beacons were also used as aids to navigation. Harris explains that these beacons were not lighthouses but "poles set in the seabed, or on the seashore, with perhaps an old lantern affixed to the top."[10] The regulation of seamarks and the provision of buoys and beacons in the early sixteenth century were the responsibility of the Lord High Admiral. To provide buoys and beacons, he appointed deputies who collected dues from ships presumed to have benefitted from the marks. In 1566 Trinity House was given the right to provide and also to regulate seamarks. It had the responsibility of seeing that privately owned seamarks were maintained. As an example, a merchant who had cut down without permission a clump of trees which had served as a seamark was upbraided for "preferring a tryfle of private benefit to your selfe before a great and generall good to the publique."[11] He could have been fined £100 (with the proceeds divided equally between the Crown and Trinity House). There seems to have been some doubt as to whether the Act of 1566 gave Trinity House the right to place seamarks in the water. This doubt was removed in 1594, when the rights of beaconage and buoyage were surrendered by the Lord High Admiral and were granted to Trinity House. How things worked out in practice is not clear, since the Lord High Admiral continued to regulate buoyage and beaconage after 1594, but gradually the authority of Trinity House in this area seems to have been acknowledged.

Early in the seventeenth century, Trinity House established lighthouses at Caister and Lowestoft.[12] But it was not until late in the century that it built another lighthouse. In the

10. Ibid., 153.
11. Ibid., 161.
12. Ibid., 183–87.

meantime the building of lighthouses had been taken over by private individuals. As Harris says: "A characteristic element in Elizabethan society were the promoters of projects advanced ostensibly for the public benefit but in reality intended for private gain. Lighthouses did not escape their attention."[13] Later he says: "With the completion of the lighthouse at Lowestoft, the Brethren rested content and did no more. . .when in February 1614 they were asked to do something positive, and erect lighthouses at Winterton in response to a petition by some three hundred shipmasters, owners and fishermen, they seem to have done nothing. Failure to respond to demands of this sort not only shook confidence in the Corporation; since there was a prospect of profit, it was tantamount to inviting private speculators to intervene. They soon did so."[14] In the period 1610–1675, no lighthouses were erected by Trinity House. At least 10 were built by private individuals.[15] Of course, the desire of private individuals to erect lighthouses put Trinity House in a quandary. On the one hand, it wanted to be recognized as the only body with authority to construct lighthouses; on the other, it was reluctant to invest its own funds in lighthouses. It therefore opposed the efforts of private individuals to construct lighthouses but, as we have seen, without success. Harris comments: "The lighthouse projectors were typical of the speculators of the period: they were not primarily motivated by considerations of public service. . . There was a strong foundation of truth in what Sir Edward Coke told Parliament in 1621 'Proiectours like wattermen looke one waye and rowe another: they pretend publique profit, intende private.' "[16] The difficulty was that those who were motivated by a sense of public service did not build lighthouses. As Harris says later: "Admittedly the primary motive of the lighthouse projectors was personal gain, but at least they got things done."[17]

13. Ibid., 180–81.
14. Ibid., 187.
15. D. Alan Stevenson, *The World's Lighthouses Before 1820* (London: Oxford University Press, 1959), 259.
16. G. G. Harris, *Trinity House*, 214.
17. Ibid., 264.

The method used by private individuals to avoid infringing Trinity House's statutory authority was to obtain a patent from the Crown which empowered them to build a lighthouse and to levy tolls on ships presumed to have benefitted from it. The way this was done was to present a petition from shipowners and shippers in which they said that they would greatly benefit from the lighthouse and were willing to pay the toll. Signatures were, I assume, obtained in the way signatures to petitions are normally obtained, but no doubt they often represented a genuine expression of opinion. The King presumably used these grants of patents on occasion as a means of rewarding those who had served him. Later, the right to operate a lighthouse and to levy tolls was granted to individuals by Acts of Parliament.

The tolls were collected at the ports by agents (who might act for several lighthouses) who might be private individuals but were commonly customs officials. The toll varied with the lighthouse and ships paid a toll, varying with the size of the vessel, for each lighthouse passed. It was normally a rate per ton (say 1/4d or 1/2d) for each voyage. Later, books were published setting out the lighthouses passed on different voyages and the charges that would be made.

In the meantime, Trinity House came to adopt a policy which maintained its rights while preserving its money (and even increasing it). Trinity House would apply for a patent to operate a lighthouse and would then grant a lease, for a rental, to a private individual who would then build the lighthouse with his own money. The advantage to a private individual of such a procedure would be that he would secure the co-operation rather than the opposition of Trinity House.

An example of this is afforded by the building, and re-building, of what is probably the most celebrated British lighthouse, the Eddystone, on a reef of rocks some 14 miles offshore from Plymouth. D. Alan Stevenson comments: "The construction of 4 lighthouses in succession on the Eddystone Rocks by 1759 provides the most dramatic chapter in lighthouse history: in striving to withstand the force of the waves, their builders showed enterprise, ingenuity and courage of a high order."[18]

18. D. Alan Stevenson, *World's Lighthouses,* 113.

In 1665, a petition for a lighthouse on the Eddystone Rocks was received by the British Admiralty. Trinity House commented that, though desirable, it "could hardly be accomplished."[19] As Samuel Smiles, that chronicler of private enterprise, says: ". . . it was long before any private adventurer was found ready to undertake so daring an enterprise as the erection of a lighthouse on the Eddystone, where only a little crest of rock was visible at high water, scarcely capable of affording foothold for a structure of the very narrowest basis."[20] In 1692, a proposal was put forward by Walter Whitfield, and Trinity House made an agreement with him under which he was to build the lighthouse and Trinity House was to share equally in whatever profits were made. Whitfield did not, however, undertake the work. His rights were transferred to Henry Winstanley, who, after negotiating with Trinity House, made an agreement in 1696 under which he was to receive the profits for the first five years, after which Trinity House was to share equally in whatever profits were earned for 50 years. Winstanley built one tower and then replaced it with another, the lighthouse being completed in 1699. However, in a great storm in 1703, the lighthouse was swept away, and Winstanley, the lighthouse-keepers, and some of his workmen lost their lives. The total cost up to this time had been £8,000 (all of which had been borne by Winstanley) and the receipts had been £4,000. The government gave Winstanley's widow £200 and a pension of £100 per annum. If the construction of lighthouses had been left solely to men with the public interest at heart, the Eddystone would have remained for a long time without a lighthouse. But the prospect of private gain once more reared its ugly head. Two men, Lovett and Rudyerd, decided to build another lighthouse. Trinity House agreed to apply for an Act of Parliament, authorizing the rebuilding and the imposition of tolls, and to lease their rights to the new builders. The terms were better than had been granted to Winstanley—a 99-year lease at an annual rent of £100 with 100 per cent of the profits going to

19. Ibid.
20. Samuel Smiles, *Lives of the Engineers,* vol. 2 (London: J. Murray, 1861), 16.

the builders. The lighthouse was completed in 1709 and remained in operation until 1755, when it was destroyed by fire. The lease still had some 50 years to run, and the interest in the lighthouse had passed into other hands. The new owners decided to rebuild and engaged one of the great engineers of the time, John Smeaton. He determined to build the lighthouse entirely of stone, the previous structure having been made of wood. The lighthouse was completed by 1759. It continued in operation until 1882, when it was replaced by a new structure built by Trinity House.[21]

We may understand the significance of the part played by private individuals and organizations in the provision of lighthouses in Britain if we consider the position at the beginning of the nineteenth century. The 1834 Committee on Lighthouses stated in their report that at that time there were in England and Wales (excluding floating lights) 42 lighthouses belonging to Trinity House; 3 lighthouses leased by Trinity House and in charge of individuals; 7 lighthouses leased by the Crown to individuals; 4 lighthouses in the hands of proprietors, held originally under patents and subsequently sanctioned by Acts of Parliament; or 56 in total, of which 14 were run by private individuals and organizations.[22] Between 1820 and 1834, Trinity House had built 9 new lighthouses, had purchased 5 lighthouses leased to individuals (in the case of Burnham, replacing the one purchased by building two lighthouses not counted in the 9 new built lighthouses), and had purchased 3 lighthouses owned by Greenwich Hospital (which acquired the lighthouses by bequest in 1719, they having been built by Sir John Meldrum about 1634). The position in 1820 was that there were 24 lighthouses operated by Trinity House and 22 by private individuals or organizations.[23] But many of the Trinity House lighthouses had not been built originally by them but had been acquired

21. This account of the building and rebuilding of the Eddystone lighthouse is based on Stevenson, *World's Lighthouses*, 113–26.

22. See Report from the Select Committee on Lighthouses, in *Parl. Papers Sess. 1834*, vol. 12, at vi (Reports from Committees, vol. 8—hereinafter cited as "1834 Report").

23. Ibid., vii.

by purchase or as the result of the expiration of a lease (of which the Eddystone Lighthouse is an example, the lease having expired in 1804). Of the 24 lighthouses operated by Trinity House in 1820, 12 had been acquired as a result of the falling in of the lease while one had been taken over from the Chester Council in 1816, so that only 11 out of the 46 lighthouses in existence in 1820 had been originally built by Trinity House, while 34 had been built by private individuals.[24]

Since the main building activity of Trinity House started at the end of the eighteenth century, the dominance of private lighthouses was even more marked in earlier periods. Writing of the position in 1786, D. A. Stevenson says: "It is difficult to assess the attitude of Trinity House towards the English coastal lighthouses at this time. Judging by its actions and not by its protestations, the determination of the Corporation to erect lighthouses had never been strong: before 1806, whenever possible it had passed on to lessees the duty of erecting them. In 1786 it controlled lighthouses at 4 places: at Caister and Lowestoft (both managed in virtue of its local buoyage dues), and at Winterton and Scilly (both erected by the Corporation to thwart individuals keen to profit from dues under Crown patents)."[25]

However, by 1834, as we have seen, there were 56 lighthouses in total and Trinity House operated 42 of them. And there was strong support in Parliament for the proposal that Trinity House purchase the remaining lighthouses in private hands. This had been suggested by a Select Committee of the House of Commons in 1822, and Trinity House began shortly afterwards to buy out certain of the private interests in light-

24. Of the 24 lighthouses operated by Trinity House in 1820, Foulness (1), Portland (2), Caskets (3), Eddystone (1), Lizard (2), St. Bees (1), and Milford (2) appear to have been acquired by the falling in of the leases and to have been built, as well as operated, by private individuals. This is based on information contained in Stevenson, *World's Lighthouses*. I have assumed, when a patent for a lighthouse was obtained by Trinity House and was then leased to a private individual, that the construction was undertaken and paid for by that individual, which appears to have been the case. See Ibid., 253, 261.

25. Ibid., 65.

houses. In 1836, an Act of Parliament vested all lighthouses in England in Trinity House, which was empowered to purchase the remaining lighthouses in private hands.[26] This was accomplished by 1842, after which date there were no longer any privately owned lighthouses, apart from "local lights," in England.

The purchase by Trinity House between 1823 and 1832 of the remainder of the leases that it had granted for Flatholm, Ferns, Burnham, and North and South Forelands cost about £74,000.[27] The rest of the private lighthouses were purchased following the 1836 Act for just under £1,200,000, the largest sums being paid for the Smalls lighthouse, for which the lease had 41 years to run, and for three lighthouses, Tynemouth, Spurn, and Skerries, for which the grant had been made in perpetuity by Act of Parliament. The sums paid for these four lighthouses were: Smalls, £170,000; Tynemouth, £125,000; Spurn, £330,000; Skerries, £445,000.[28] These are large sums, the £445,000 paid for Skerries being equivalent (according to a high authority) to $7–10 million today, which would probably have produced (owing to the lower level of taxation) a considerably higher income than today. Thus we find examples of men who were not only, in Samuelson's words, "odd enough to try to make a fortune running a lighthouse business," but actually succeeded in doing so.

The reasons why there was such strong support for this consolidation of lighthouses in the hands of Trinity House can be learned from the Report of the Select Committee of the House of Commons of 1834:

> Your Committee have learned with some surprise that the Lighthouse Establishments have been conducted in the several parts of the United Kingdom under entirely different systems; different as regards the con-

---

26. An Act for Vesting Lighthouse, Lights and Sea Marks on the Coasts of England in the Corporation of Trinity House of Deptford Strond, 6 & 7 Will. 4, ch. 79 (1836).

27. "1834 Report," at vii.

28. Report from the Select Committee on Lighthouses, in *Parl. Papers Sess. 1845*, vol. 9, at vi (hereinafter cited as "1845 Report").

stitution of the Boards of Management, different as regards the Rates or Amount of the Light Dues, and different in the principle on which they are levied. They have found that these Establishments, of such importance to the extensive Naval and Commercial Interests in the Kingdom, instead of being conducted under the immediate superintendence of the Government, upon one uniform system, and under responsible Public Servants, with proper foresight to provide for the safety of the Shipping in the most efficient manner, and on the most economical plans, have been left to spring up, as it were by slow degrees, as the local wants required, often after disastrous losses at sea; and it may, perhaps, be considered as matter of reproach to this great country, that for ages past, as well as at the present time, a considerable portion of the establishments of lighthouses have been made the means of heavily taxing the Trade of the country, for the benefit of a few private individuals, who have been favoured with that advantage by the Ministers and the Sovereign of the day.

Your Committee cannot consider it warrantable in Government, at any time, unnecessarily to tax any branch of the Industry of the Country; and particularly unwarrantable to tax the Shipping, which lies under many disadvantages, in being obliged to support unequal competition with the Shipping of other countries. Your Committee are of opinion that the Shipping ought, on very special grounds, to be relieved from every local and unequal tax not absolutely necessary for the services for which it is ostensibly levied.

Your Committee, therefore, strongly recommend that the Light Dues should in every case be reduced to the smallest sums requisite to maintain the existing Lighthouses and Floating Lights, or to establish and maintain such new Establishments as shall be required for the benefit of the Commerce and Shipping of the country.

Your Committee have, further, to express their regret that so little attention should have been paid by the competent authorities to the continued exaction, contrary to the principle just expressed, of very large sums which have been annually levied, avowedly, as Light Dues, to defray the expenses of Lighthouses but, in reality, to be applied to the use of a few favoured individuals, and for other purposes not contemplated at the time of the establishment of the Lighthouses. It further appears particularly objectionable to have continued these abuses by the renewal of the Leases of several Lighthouses, after a Select Committee of this House had called the particular attention of Parliament, 12 years ago, to the subject. . . .[29]

Although there was emphasis in this report on the untidiness of the then existing arrangements and suggestions (here and elsewhere) that some of the private lighthouses were not run efficiently, there can be little doubt that the main reason why the consolidation of lighthouses under Trinity House received such strong support was that it was thought that it would lead to lower light dues. The suggestion was, of course, made that lighthouses should be paid for out of the public treasury,[30] which would lead to the abolition of light dues, but this was not done and we need not discuss it here.

It is not apparent why it was thought that the consolidation of lighthouses under Trinity House would lower light dues. There is some basis for this view in the theory of complementary monopolies, but Cournot did not publish his analysis until 1838, and it could not have affected the views of those concerned with British lighthouses even if they were quicker to appreciate the significance of Cournot's analysis than the economics profession itself.[31] In any case, there were good reasons for thinking that little, if any, reduction in light dues would

29. "1834 Report," at iii–iv.

30. For example, the Select Committee on Lighthouses of 1845 recommended "That all expenses for the erection and maintenance of Lighthouses . . . be henceforth defrayed out of the public revenue. . . ." See the "1845 Report," at xii.

31. See Augustin Cournot, *Researches into the Mathematical Principles of the Theory of Wealth*, trans. Nathaniel T. Bacon (New York: Macmillan Co., 1897), 99–104. See also Alfred Marshall's discussion of Cournot's analysis in *Principles of Economics*, vol. 1, 9th (variorum) ed. (London: Macmillan for the Royal Economic Society, 1961), 493–95.

follow the consolidation. Since compensation was to be paid to the former owners of lighthouses, the same amount of money would need to be raised as before. And, as was pointed out by Trinity House, since "the Dues were mortgaged as security for the repayment of the money borrowed . . . the Dues cannot be taken off until the debt shall be discharged."[32] In fact, the light dues were not reduced until after 1848, when the loans were paid off.[33]

Another way in which some reduction in light dues could have been achieved would have been for Trinity House not to earn a net income from the operation of its own lighthouses. This money was, of course, devoted to charitable purposes, mainly the support of retired seamen and their widows and orphans. Such a use of funds derived ultimately from the light dues had been found objectionable by Parliamentary Committees in 1822 and 1834. The 1834 Committee, noting that 142 persons were supported in almshouses and that 8,431 men, women, and children received sums ranging from 36 shillings to 30 pounds per annum, proposed that all pensions cease with the lives of those then receiving them and that no new pensioners be appointed, but this was not done.[34]

In 1853, the Government proposed that the proceeds of the light dues no longer be used for charitable purposes. Trinity House responded, in a representation to Her Majesty, claiming that this income was as much its property as it had been for private proprietors of lighthouses (to whom compensation was paid):

> The management of lighthouses has been entrusted to [TrinityHouse], from time to time, by special grants from the Crown or the Legislature. But the acceptance of such grants has in no respect changed the legal position of the Corporation as a private guild, except in so far as it has necessitated the maintenance of lights as a condition of retaining such grants. The legal po-

32. "1845 Report," at vii.
33. T. Golding, *Trinity House from Within* (London: Smith & Ibbs, 1929), 63.
34. "1834 Report," at xiii.

sition of the Corporation with regard to the Crown and the public has in no respect differed from that of individual grantees of light dues or other franchises, as markets, ports, fairs, etc. The argument that the Corporation was ever legally bound to reduce the light dues to the amount of the expenses of maintenance, inclusive or exclusive of interest on the cost of erection, and that they had no right to make any other appropriation, is altogether unfounded in reason or law . . . a grant is valid, if the dues granted are reasonable at the time of the grant, and continues so valid, notwithstanding that from a subsequent increase of shipping the dues may afford a profit. The Crown in these cases acts on behalf of the public; and if it makes a bargain, reasonable at the time, it cannot afterwards retract. . . . The title of the Corporation to the lighthouse erected by them is equally valid with the titles [of private proprietors] . . . and the charitable purposes to which a portion of those revenues is applied, render the claims of the Corporation at least as deserving of favourable consideration as those of individuals. . . . The lighthouses and light dues belong to [Trinity House], for the purposes of the Corporation, and are, in the strictest sense, their property for those purposes. . . The proposal of Her Majesty's Government appears to be that the use of the whole of this vast mass of property shall be given to the shipowners, without any charge beyond the expense of maintaining the lights. It is, as affecting the Corporation's charities, an alienation of property, devoted to the benefit of the decayed masters and seamen of the merchant's service, and their families, and a gift of that property to the shipowners.[35]

The representation was referred to the Board of Trade, which found the arguments of Trinity House without merit:

---

35. Trinity House Charities: Representation from the Corporation of the Trinity House to Her Majesty in Council, on proposal of Government to prevent the Application of Light and Other Dues to Charitable Purposes, in *Parl. Papers Sess. 1852–53*, vol. 98: 601, 602–03.

The Lords of the Committee do not call in question the title of the Corporation of the Trinity House to the property so alleged to be vested in them; but there is . . . this distinction between the case of the Corporation and that of the individuals referred to, that the property so vested in the Corporation has been held and is held by them, so far at least as relates to the light dues in question, in trust for public purposes, and liable, therefore, to be dealt with upon consideration of public policy. Their Lordships cannot admit that is any violation of the principle of property in the reduction of a tax levied for public purposes, where no vested interests have been acquired in the proceeds of the tax; and where the tax in question is one levied upon a particular class of Your Majesty's subjects, without that class deriving any adequate advantage in return (and any excess of light dues beyond the amount necessary to maintain the lights is a tax of this character), the reduction of such a tax not only involves no violation of the principle of property, but is in the highest degree just and expedient. Their Lordships cannot recognise any vested interests in the expectants of the bounty dealt out to poor mariners and their families, at the pleasure of the Corporation, from the surplus revenues of the lights; since it is of the essence of a vested interest that the individuals to whom the privilege is secured are ascertained and known to the law; and while their Lordships would religiously abstain from interfering in the slightest degree with the pensions or other benefits already conferred upon any person whatsoever, they can acknowledge no injustice in resolving, upon grounds of public policy, to confer upon no new persons a right, to which at present no individual can advance any claim or title. . . . Their Lordships consider that the lights should be maintained by the light dues; and that what the providence of former generations has done in applying dues levied upon ships to the erection of lights for the preservation of ships from shipwreck, is the natural and just inheritance of those who navigate the coasts of the United Kingdom at the present time, and ought to be freely enjoyed by them at the lowest possible charge which the circumstances of the case may permit, and that no other consideration whatever should on any account be suffered to enter into the question.[36]

The use of the proceeds of the light dues for charitable purposes ceased in 1853. As a result, some reduction in the light dues was made possible, price moved closer to marginal cost, and numerous ancient mariners and their families, unknown to the law and to us, were worse provided for. But it will be observed that it was not necessary to have a consolidation of all lighthouses under Trinity House to bring about this result.

This change was part of the reorganization which, in 1853, established the Mercantile Marine Fund, into which the light dues (and certain other monies) were paid and out of which the expense of running the lighthouse service and some other expenses incurred on behalf of shipping were met.[37] In 1898, the system was again changed. The Mercantile Marine Fund was abolished and the General Lighthouse Fund was set up. The light dues (and only the light dues) were paid into this fund, which was to be used solely for the maintenance of the lighthouse service. At the same time, the system for computing the light dues was simplified, the charge made on each voyage no longer depending, as it had before, on the number of lighthouses which a ship passed or from which it could be presumed to derive a benefit.[38] What was established in 1898 was essen-

36. Ibid., 605–06.
37. The Merchant Shipping Law Amendment Act of 1853, 16 & 17 Vict., ch. 131 §§ 3–30.
38. Merchant Shipping (Mercantile Marine Fund) Act of 1898, 61 & 62 Vict., ch. 44. See the "Committee of Inquiry into the Mercantile Marine Fund, Report Cd. No. 8167 (1896)," also found in *Parl. Papers Sess. 1896,* vol. 41, at 113, for the reasons why this change was made in the way light dues were computed. The recommendations of this Committee were adopted by the Government and were incorporated in the 1898 Act. Objections to the old system arose because the list of lighthouses from which ships were presumed to benefit on a given voyage was based on the course of a sailing ship rather than that of a steamship, and because the foreign rate was charged to the last port reached in the United Kingdom in the course of a voyage and not to the first, while much was made of the complexity of the old method of calculating the dues.

tially the present system of lighthouse finance and administration described in section II. There have, of course, been changes in detail, but the general character of the system has remained the same since 1898.

IV. Conclusion

The sketch of the British lighthouse system and its evolution in sections II and III shows how limited are the lessons to be drawn from the remarks of Mill, Sidgwick, and Pigou. Mill seems to be saying that if something like the British system for the finance and administration of lighthouses is not instituted, private operation of lighthouses would be impossible (which is not how most modern readers would be likely to interpret him). Sidgwick and Pigou argue that if there are ships which benefit from the lighthouse but on which tolls cannot be levied, then governmental intervention may be called for. But the ships which benefit from British lighthouses but do not pay would presumably be, in the main, those operated by foreign shipowners which do not call at British ports. In which case, it is not clear what the character of the required governmental action is or what governments are supposed to act. Should, for example, the Russian, Norwegian, German, and French governments compel their nationals to pay the toll even though their ships do not call at British ports, or should these governments take action by paying a sum raised out of general taxation into the British General Lighthouse Fund? Or is the British government supposed to take action by raising revenue out of general taxation to be paid into the Lighthouse Fund to offset the failure of these foreign governments to compel their nationals to contribute to the Lighthouse Fund?

Now consider what would be likely to happen if support out of general taxation were substituted for the light dues (which seems to be what Samuelson would like). First of all, it would increase the extent to which the British Government, and particularly the Treasury, would feel obliged to supervise the operations of the lighthouse service in order to keep under control the amount of the subsidy. This intervention of the Treasury would tend to reduce somewhat the efficiency with which the lighthouse service was administered. And it would have another effect. Because the revenue is now raised from the consumers of the service, a committee has been established, the Lights Advisory Committee, representing Shipowners, Underwriters, and Shippers, which is consulted about the budget, the operations of the service, and particularly about new works. In this way, the lighthouse service is made more responsive to those who make use of its service; and because it is the shipping industry which actually pays for additional services, they will presumably support changes in the arrangements only when the value of the additional benefits received is greater than the cost. This administrative arrangement would presumably be discarded if the service were financed out of general taxation, and the service would therefore become somewhat less efficient. The Chairman of the 1896 Committee of Inquiry into the Mercantile Marine Fund was Leonard Courtney, M. P. Courtney, who was an economist, made essentially the same point in the debate in the House of Commons. Replying to those who had suggested that the lighthouse service should be supported out of general taxation, Courtney commented: ". . . there is one substantial argument in favour of our maintaining the service as it is, and that is that there is an impression among shipowners—and it is a very useful one—that they have to bear the burden, and they are extremely jealous of the expenditure, and they would claim hereafter, if not now, a share in the administration; that is to say, that they being the people called upon to pay in the first instance, scrutinise the expenditure in which they are interested, and jealously guard it. This is a great advantage, and I conceive that by it economy and efficiency in the coast light service are obtained, and I think that to change a system which secures a frugal and yet sufficient administration of the service would be most inexpedient. The shipowners are jealously watching the whole of the administration, and they claim, I think justly, to have a voice in the matter conceded them. If the cost of lighting the coasts were thrown directly upon the Votes every year, there would not be the same check as is now existing upon unbounded demands which might be made in those ebullitions of feeling to which the nation is always exposed after some great maritime calamity."[39]

In general it would seem to be a safe conclusion that the move to support the lighthouse service out of general taxation would result in a less appropriate administrative structure. And what is the gain which Samuelson sees as coming from this change in the way in which the lighthouse service is financed? It is that some ships which are now discouraged from making a voyage to Britain because of the light dues would in future do so. As it happens, the form of the toll and the exemptions mean that for most ships the number of voyages will not be affected by the fact that light dues are paid. There is no further liability for light dues after the first ten voyages in a year for "home-trade" ships and the first six voyages for "foreign-going" ships. It seems to be the opinion of those conversant with the shipping industry that the vast majority of ships will not need to pay light dues on their last voyages in the year. A cross-channel ferry could probably meet the requisite number of journeys in a few days. Ships trading with Europe or North America will normally not be required to pay light dues on their last voyages. However, the ships trading with Australia will usually not be able to complete the number of voyages necessary to avoid light dues. There may be some ships somewhere which are laid up or broken up because of the light dues, but the number cannot be great, if indeed there are any ships in this category.[40] It is difficult for me to resist the conclusion

39. 40 Parl. Deb. (4th ser.) 186–87 (1898). That is to say, Courtney was arguing that the method of finance meant that the shipowners were led to exercise at this early date the same influence over expenditures as is now exercised through the Lights Advisory Committee.

40. I have not been able to secure any precise figures, but all indications are that light dues form a very small proportion of the costs of running a ship trading with the United Kingdom. Such statistics as exist support this view. Payments into the General Lighthouse Fund in 1971–1972 were £8,900,000. General Lighthouse Fund 1971–1972, H. C. Paper No. 301 (in cont. of H. C. Paper No. 211), at 2 (July 3, 1973). In 1971, the earnings of ships owned by U.K. operators and of ships on charter to them for carrying U.K. imports and exports, visitors to the U.K., and U.K. residents were about £700 million. In addition, about £50 million was earned in the U.K. coastal trade. Payments

that the benefit which would come from the abandonment of the light dues would be very unimportant and that there would be some loss from the change in the administrative structure.

The question remains: How is it that these great men have, in their economic writings, been led to make statements about lighthouses which are misleading as to the facts, whose meaning, if thought about in a concrete fashion, is quite unclear, and which, to the extent that they imply a policy conclusion, are very likely wrong? The explanation is that these references by economists to lighthouses are not the result of their having made a study of lighthouses or having read a detailed study by some other economist. Despite the extensive use of the lighthouse example in the literature, no economist, to my knowledge, has ever made a comprehensive study of lighthouse finance and administration. The lighthouse is simply plucked out of the air to serve as an illustration. The purpose of the lighthouse example is to provide "corroborative detail, intended to give artistic verisimilitude to an otherwise bald and unconvincing narrative."[41]

This seems to me to be the wrong approach. I think we should try to develop generalizations which would give us guidance as to how various activities should best be organized and financed. But such generalizations are not likely to be helpful unless they are derived from studies of how such activities are actually carried out within different institutional frameworks. Such studies would enable us to discover which factors are important and which are not in determining the outcome, and they would lead to generalizations which have a solid base. They are also likely to serve another purpose by showing us

---

to foreign shipowners for carrying U.K. imports and exports were probably of the order of £600 million in 1971. This suggests that the annual costs of running ships trading with the U.K. must have been about £1,400 million. These estimates are based on figures kindly supplied to me by the Department of Trade. Some of the separate figures brought together to obtain these totals are very rough estimates but they give the order of magnitude, and whatever error they contain would not affect the conclusion that payments into the General Lighthouse Fund form a very small proportion of the cost of running a ship trading with the U.K.

41. William S. Gilbert, "The Mikado."

the richness of the social alternatives among which we can choose.

The account in this paper of the British system does little more than reveal some of the possibilities. The early history shows that, contrary to the belief of many economists, a lighthouse service can be provided by private enterprise. In those days, shipowners and shippers could petition the Crown to allow a private individual to construct a lighthouse and to levy a (specified) toll on ships benefitting from it. The lighthouses were built, operated, financed, and owned by private individuals, who could sell a lighthouse or dispose of it by bequest. The role of the government was limited to the establishment and enforcement of property rights in the lighthouse. The charges were collected at the ports by agents for the lighthouses. The problem of enforcement was no different for them than for other suppliers of goods and services to the shipowner. The property rights were unusual only in that they stipulated the price that could be charged.[42]

42. This arrangement avoided a problem raised by Arrow in discussing the lighthouse example. Arrow says: "In my view, the standard lighthouse example is best analyzed as a problem of small numbers rather than of the difficulty of exclusion though both elements are present. To simplify matters, I will abstract from uncertainty so that the lighthouse keeper knows exactly when each ship will need its service, and also abstract from indivisibility (since the light is either on or off). Assume further that only one ship will be within range of the lighthouse at any moment. Then exclusion is perfectly possible; the lighthouse need only shut off its light when a nonpaying ship is coming into range. But there would be only one buyer and one seller and no competitive forces to drive the two into a competitive equilibrium. If in addition the costs of bargaining are high, then it may be most efficient to offer the service free." See Kenneth J. Arrow, "The Organization of Economic Activity: Issues Pertinent to the Choice of Market Versus Nonmarket Allocation," in U.S. Cong., Jt. Econ. Comm., Subcomm. on Economy in Government, 91st Cong., 1st Sess., *The Analysis and Evaluation of Public Expenditures: the PPB System,* vol. 1, at 47, 58 (J. Comm. Print 1969). Arrow's surrealist picture of a lighthouse keeper shutting off the light as soon as it became useful while arguing with the captain about the charge to be made (assuming that the vessel has not run on the rocks in the meantime) bears no relation to the situation faced by those responsible for lighthouse policy. In Britain, no negotiation has been required to determine individual charges and no lighthouse keeper has ever turned off the light for this purpose. Arrow's conclusion that "it may be most efficient to offer the service free" is unexceptionable but also unhelpful since it is equally true that it may not.

Later, the provision of lighthouses in England and Wales was entrusted to Trinity House, a private organization with public duties, but the service continued to be financed by tolls levied on ships. The system apparently favoured by Samuelson, finance by the government out of general taxation, has never been tried in Britain. Such a government-financed system does not necessarily exclude the participation of private enterprise in the building or operation of lighthouses, but it would seem to preclude private ownership of lighthouses, except in a very attenuated form, and would certainly be quite different from the system in Britain which came to an end in the 1830s. Of course, government finance would be very likely to involve both government operation and government ownership of lighthouses. How such governmental systems actually operate I do not know. Bierce's definition of an American lighthouse—"A tall building on the seashore in which the government maintains a lamp and the friend of a politician"[43]—presumably does not tell the whole story.

We may conclude that economists should not use the lighthouse as an example of a service which could only be provided by the government. But this paper is not intended to settle the question of how lighthouse service ought to be organized and financed. This must await more detailed studies. In the meantime, economists wishing to point to a service which is best provided by the government should use an example which has a more solid backing.

43. Ambrose Bierce, *The Devil's Dictionary,* (New York: A. & C. Boni, 1925), 193.

Index

Adams v. Ursell, 123
Adelman, Morris A., 67
Andreae v. Selfridge and Company Ltd., 124–28
Arrow, Kenneth J., 212n42
Auten, Gerald E., 164–65
Average cost pricing, 90–92

Bain, Joe S., 59, 60
Bass v. Gregory, 112–14
Batt, Francis R., 39n20, 54
Baumol, William J., 179–85
Becker, Gary S., 2–3
Bierce, Ambrose, 213
"Blackboard economics," 28–30
Bland v. Yates, 146
Bonbright, James C., 76n4
Boulston v. Hardy, 144–45, 146–47
Bramwell, L. J., 109
Bray, J., 145
Brozen, Yale, 69
Bryant v. Lefever, 109–13

Cannan, Edwin, 85n23, 134
Caves, Richard, 60
Cheung, Steven N. S., 15
Choice, analysis of, 2–3
Clark, J. B., 35
Clemens, E. W., 76
Coase theorem, 13–15, 157–60, 163–70, 173, 174
Cooke v. Forbes, 107–8
Cost curve of the firm, 51–53
Cotton, L. J., 110

Cournot, Augustin, 203
Courtney, Leonard, 209, 210n29

Dahlman, Carl J., 6
Dawes, Harry, 38n15
Delta Air Corporation v. Kersey, Kersey v. City of Atlanta, 128–30
Denning, Sir Alfred, 131
Dobb, Maurice, 36, 46n31, 47
Durbin, E. F. M., 37n14

Economic analysis, Pigovian tradition and, 20–30, 149–53
Economic system, and the firm, 34–37
Economic theory of politics, 70
Economics, nature of, 1–2
Edgeworth, F. Y., 160, 162
Employer/employee relationship, and the nature of the firm, 53–55
Entrepreneurship, 36n10
Exchange, theory of, 2–5
Externalities, defined, 23–24

Fabricant, Solomon, 72
Firm, 5–7; defined, 3, 33–34; nature of the, 33–55
Fleming, J. M., 16, 75, 76, 77, 90
Forte, Francesco, 142–43
Frisch, Ragnar, 76n5, 88
Fuchs, Victor, 59n2
Futures markets, 10n12

Georgia Railroad and Banking Co. v. Maddox, 129

Gort, Michael, 72, 73
Government, economic activities of, 70, 187–213
Green, Sir Wilfred, 124

Hahn, Frank, 5–6, 23–24
Harris, G. G., 196
Havlik, H. F., 81n–82n, 93
Hotelling, H., 16, 75, 76nn4–5, 77–78, 82–93

Industrial organization, research proposal on, 57
Inventions, and the price mechanism, 46n31

Jones, Eliot, 43n26

Kaldor, Nicholas, 38n18, 46n29
Keynes, John Maynard, 16
Knight, Frank H., 4, 35, 40–42, 48–51, 154

Labor, division of, and the firm, 47–51
Law, and the economic system, 10–16
Lerner, A. P., 16, 75, 77, 82–93
Liability for damage, and the pricing system, 97–104
Lighthouse system, British, 191–213

McGee, John S., 67
Macgregor, D. H., 43n26
Marginal cost, 75–93
Marginal cost pricing, 16–20
Markets, 7–10
Market transaction costs, and social cost, 114–19
Marshall, Alfred, 7, 21, 34, 35, 61
Master/servant relationship, and the nature of the firm, 53–55
Meade, J. E., 16, 29, 75, 77, 83, 84, 90
Mill, John Stuart, 29, 187, 190–91, 194, 208

Monopoly, and industrial organization, 66–69
Multipart pricing, 80–82

National Bureau of Economic Research, 57–58, 71–73
Nelson, Ralph L., 72, 73

Optimum pricing, 79–80
Optimum size of the firm, theory of, 64–65

Paine, C. L., 76
Peterman, John L., 67
Pigou, A. C., 95, 159, 175, 179, 188, 190–91, 208; and modern economic analysis, 20–30; and the problem of social cost, 133–49
Pigovian taxes, 179–85
Pigovian tradition, 149–53
Politics, economic theory of, 70
Price mechanism, 35–37
Price theory, 2–5
Pricing, 75–93; average cost, 90–92; multipart, 80–82; optimum, 79–80
Pricing system, and damage liability, 97–104

Rationalization, 43n26
Regan, Donald H., 164
Rex v. Ronkett, 120n16
Rights: assignment of, 170–74; legal delimitation of, and social cost, 119–33
Robbins, Lionel, 1–2, 36
Robertson, D. H., 35, 61, 62
Robinson, E. A. G., 22, 43n26, 46n29, 46n30, 51n43, 51–52n44, 61
Robinson, Joan, 33, 51, 53
Rushman v. Polsue and Alfieri, Ltd., 123n24

Salter, Sir Arthur, 34–35, 62
Samuelson, Paul A., 17, 23, 29, 30, 159–63, 188–90, 210
Shove, G. F., 38n17, 53
Sidgwick, Henry, 188, 190–91, 194, 208
Slater, Martin, 3
Smith, Adam, 9, 36, 65, 134n38
Smith v. New England Aircraft Co., 130–31
Social cost, 10–16, 95–156, 157–85
Specialized exchange economy, emergence of firm in, 37–40
Stephen, Sir James Fitzjames, 120n16
Stevenson, D. Alan, 197, 200
Stigler, George J., 14, 59, 60, 65, 96, 157–58
Sturges v. Bridgman, 105–8, 111, 122, 157, 174

Taxes, Pigovian, 179–85
Thorp, Willard, 61, 73

Thrasher v. City of Atlanta, 128
Transactions costs, influence of, 174–79

Usher, Abbott, 39n19, 47

von Thunen, J. H., 52

Wealth: distribution of, 170–74; maximization of, 159–63
Webb v. Bird, 121–23
Wellisz, Stanislaw, 164
Whitfield, Walter, 198
Williams, Glanville L., 144n49, 145–46
Wilson, Tom, 18, 77
Winstanley, Henry, 198

Zerbe, Richard O., Jr., 178